Local Architecture

LOCAL ARCHITECTURE

BUILDING PLACE, CRAFT, AND COMMUNITY

Brian MacKay-Lyons,
Edited by Robert McCarter

Princeton Architectural Press, New York

Contents

You brought together some wonderful people and that alone as friends should have been enough to make my visit very special. But the caliber of architecture brought together made this one of the most memorable events that I have been a part of through a career of some fifty years. It was marvelous. Thank you.

—Glenn Murcutt

I have attended numerous conferences around the world but I can say that this was the best; I was particularly impressed and inspired by the sense of optimism.

—Juhani Pallasmaa

What can I say? What can anyone say? An unrepeatable, memorable event, and a wild party.

—Kenneth Frampton

Foreword

Brian MacKay-Lyons

Don't let the school stand in the way of your education.
—Essy Baniassad

In 1994 I was an angry young architect and professor at Dalhousie University in Halifax, Nova Scotia, frustrated with the state of architectural education. I took a small group of first-year students out of school and to my farm on the Nova Scotia coast and told them: "Close your eyes and imagine flying over the ghost of a forgotten village at the end of the earth. If you breathe deeply enough you may even smell the laundry that used to hang on the clotheslines." Norwegian architecture critic Ingerid Helsing Almaas has pointed out that anger is not enough to explain the work that followed, at Ghost Architecture Laboratory and at MacKay-Lyons Sweetapple Architects. Ghost has evolved into an international design-build internship, reinforcing students' sound intuition that architecture has always been about landscape, making, and community. Ghost is also a utopian endeavor, driven by empathy and love.

After decades of cultivating our little valley at the end of the earth, the site (according to Glenn Murcutt) has become a kind of paradise. It is an optimistic act of will. It is the place that, for me, expresses the unity of life, integrating practice and teaching, family and community. For a group of friends and respected colleagues, it has been neutral turf, like Constantinos Doxiadis's boat that the Team 10 architects sailed together in the Mediterranean so many decades ago.

From the start, Ghost has not been alone. Friends such as Samuel Mockbee of the Rural Studio, Steve Badanes of Jersey Devil, and the Glenn Murcutt Master Class have been fellow travelers on this alternative dirt road. As a young architect in 1982, at Team 10 architect Giancarlo De Carlo's ILAUD (International Laboratory of Architecture and Urban Design), I witnessed a similar, collegial, alternative think tank frequented by Alison and Peter Smithson, Aldo van Eyck, Sverre Fehn, Richard Rogers, Charles Moore, Italo Calvino, and others. And Ghost has inspired other programs in its turn.

Ghost has been sustained by a loose consortium of architectural schools and practices, whose students, professors, and practicing architects and engineers have participated. It has also been a meeting place for a group of guest architects and critics, who share a commitment to the timeless architectural values of place, craft, and community—a fantastic "virtual faculty."

Ghost 13 was a long-planned reunion of past guests; a group of exceptionally talented architects and historians/critics. Place, craft, and community served as a thematic structure for the conference; the work of all of these architects is an artful synthesis of these essential aspects of our discipline. In her talk, Brigitte Shim linked the conference venues with these common values, describing the Ghost site as a cultivated place, St. John's carpenter Gothic church in Lunenburg as the embodiment of craft, and the collegial gathering in the barn as the expression of community. This was trying to see the world whole.

The three keynote speakers are respected elders who continue to influence generations of architects. Kenneth Frampton's critical regionalist thesis has enabled our resistance in the face of the numbing cultural influence of globalization. Glenn Murcutt's work, in the words of Juhani Pallasmaa, projects a new concept of beauty arising from a deep understanding of place, climate, and nature. Juhani's eloquent insistence, through his seminal writings, on the phenomenological architecture of human experience has inspired us all. At Ghost 13 the steady hand and presence of the elders contributed a measured and thoughtful rhythm to the proceedings.

Many of the participants are former outsiders, what Peter Buchanan calls "the resistance," working outside the centers of architectural fashion.

At the end of the day, all of the speakers were invited because of their high level of formal, professional design skill, as evidenced by a mature and consistent body of built work, as well as their past connection to Ghost. They speak from the authority of practice. It is important to add that this is not an exclusive group. Other like-minded architects are part of this community of respected colleagues.

Most of us are both practitioners and academics, at a time when this distinguished dual-career tradition in architecture has almost become extinct. Long gone are the days when architects, such as Walter Gropius, Louis Kahn, and Rafael Moneo, led schools. In the academy, the research culture of the sciences and the humanities is being applied to architecture—an alarming trend for an applied discipline. (In an applied nature, architecture resembles medicine or music.) The attendant promotion criteria have led a generation of young professors away from practice, with the result that design studio is now largely taught by nondesigners. The academy is becoming more esoteric. Meanwhile, in corporate practice, the educational responsibility of apprenticeship within the master builder tradition is being lost. Young architects are progressively regarded as mobile human capital, an attitude exacerbated by the use of digital production tools. Practice is becoming more anti-intellectual.

Given these circumstances, it is not surprising that architectural education was an unstated theme of Ghost 13—the elephant in the room, in fact. We oppose the unwholesome gulf between the academy and practice, between the mind and the hand. As for me, I have embraced the position of both the architect and the teacher. As a practitioner, I would like to think of myself as a farmer, whose cultivating influence on the landscape may leave the world a little richer than I found it. As a teacher I would like to think of myself as a village priest, a keeper of the faith, keeping the lamp lit in the face of often-disappointing reality.

In architecture, good intentions, while essential, are not enough. To borrow Glenn Murcutt's words on sustainability: "First it must be good architecture."

Seeing the World Whole

Thomas Fisher

"I'm just trying to see the world whole," says Brian MacKay-Lyons, capturing in one sentence the crux of what made his Ghost Architectural Laboratory so significant as an educational experiment and as a critique of beginning design curriculum. "Ghost started out of my frustration with architectural education," adds MacKay-Lyons. "I almost quit architecture school after I started. I went into architecture thinking that it would deal with the landscape, with making things, with community, which it didn't. The street outside was more interesting than what was going on in the studio."

Despite such misgivings, MacKay-Lyons finished his bachelor of architecture at the Technical University of Nova Scotia and went on to receive a master of architecture from UCLA, after which he returned to Halifax to teach. There he discovered that "faculty meetings are never about content, never talking about why we are doing this." Those experiences led him to start the two-week summer design/build program that he dubbed the "Ghost Lab." The program was located on farmland in Lower Kingsburg, Nova Scotia, amid ruins of houses near the first French settlements in North America, established by Samuel de Champlain in 1604.[1] "I started Ghost," he says, "because first-year students needed to know that they are right, that architecture is about landscape, making things, and community" instead of what he sees as all too common in our schools: the separation of the mind from the hand and of the academy from the world around it.

Ghost 13

As architectural education has become "less about making things," says MacKay-Lyons, we need to return to "the idea of making architecture out of local materials and local labor and making it affordable." At the same time, he does not believe students can "learn to design with hammer in hand. They need a degree of distance from the job site, and to learn that the role of the architect is not to be the builder, but to be the designer." As the culmination of a dozen Ghost Labs, Ghost 13 indirectly addressed this pedagogical conundrum.

At the symposium, for example, Rick Joy asked, "What should we teach?"[2] MacKay-Lyons responded with his "one-room schoolhouse approach to architectural education, in which there would be just three courses: one about place, dealing with the environment, landscape, and urbanism; one about craft, addressing technology, making, and material culture; and one about community, including clients, culture, and social agency." That three-part pedagogy formed the structure of Ghost 13. Each day of the symposium focused on one of those topics—place, craft, and community—under the overarching theme of "Ideas in Things."[3]

Place

That lesson came through clearly in the stellar lineup of designers that MacKay-Lyons assembled for the conference. After the opening keynote address by Kenneth Frampton on the role of place-based architecture as a form of resistance to globalism, architects Rick Joy, Ted Flato, Wendell Burnette, Deborah Berke, and Marlon Blackwell, along with historian Robert McCarter, discussed the influence of place on their architecture. Some of them practice far from the main centers of architectural production, in cities like Tucson, San Antonio, and Fayetteville, although Burnette's office in Phoenix and Berke's office in New York City counter the claim that MacKay-Lyons made, with his usual self-deprecating sense of humor, that "we're all boonies architects."[4] All of them, though, demonstrated, through their work, how great buildings help define and create the context in which they stand, to reveal the nature of a place that was often unappreciated before the architecture made it visible.

Paradoxically, the popularity of these architects has brought them commissions far from their offices, which has also led them to alter the forms and materials they commonly use. Rick Joy's shingled and fieldstone house in New England, for example, was quite different from the rammed-earth and Cor-ten steel he employs in Arizona. These diverse commissions, however, showed how place-specific architecture may be the only way to engage globalization in a sustainable and culturally appropriate way.

Craft

The second keynote speaker, Juhani Pallasmaa, reinforced that idea, writing:

> In the Age of Ecology, the concept of "form" has to be seen as a temporal process, or emergent situation, rather than a closed and finite aesthetic entity....I do not support any romantic bio-morphic architecture. I advocate an architecture that arises from a respect of nature in its complexity...and from empathy and loyalty to all forms of life and a humility about our own destiny.[5]

Such sentiments show how the battle lines of architectural education have been redrawn. Instead of the late twentieth-century division between a formalist avant-garde

Ghost 13 speakers gather outside of the Barn for a team photo.

and a nostalgic rear guard, we now have a divide between those who continue to design for what Pallasmaa calls "the obsessive ideal of perpetual growth…[and] the suicidal course of industrial civilizations" and those who believe that our "daily practices and education ha[ve] to be fundamentally re-evaluated…giv[ing] up the hubris of regarding ourselves as the centerpiece of the universe, and as the homo sapiens who know."[6]

That division creates a dilemma for architects, evident in the talks during the conference's second day. Architects Patricia Patkau, Peter Stutchbury, Brigitte Shim, Vincent James and Jennifer Yoos, and Tom Kundig each presented exquisite and often very expensive houses as examples of the quality and quantity of craft still possible in today's construction. The wealth required to fund such work, though, has largely arisen from the global economy's concentration of money and power in the hands of a relatively few, placing our profession in the awkward position of depending on the profits of perpetual growth even as we recognize the unsustainability of this model. And yet, the work these architects showed offered a way past that dilemma. Their attention to the craft of construction applies as much to modest houses as it does to megamansions, making the issue not about economics, but instead about ethics and the existential act of humans "improving the world rather than using it up," as MacKay-Lyons called it.

Historian Peter Buchanan addressed the question of whether the beautifully crafted buildings of these architects represented a new "arts and crafts" and whether that aligned or conflicted with the growing use of digital design and fabrication. Most participants refused to polarize these issues. As MacKay-Lyons said, "It's always 'both-and': both digital and analog, mind and hand, past and future."

Jennifer Yoos and Vincent James of VJAA walk the grounds of the Nova Scotia site for Ghost 13.

Community

In the third keynote, Glenn Murcutt confronted the issue of professional responsibility by observing that it primarily rests with doing great architecture. MacKay-Lyons underscored that later when he said: "Architecture needs both artists and activists, but every architect has to decide which is primary and which is secondary." The architect-educators who spoke on the final day of the conference had clearly decided that question. Andrew Freear, Dan Rockhill, Steve Badanes, Richard Kroeker, and Brian MacKay-Lyons all provided moving and, at times, highly entertaining accounts of their efforts, mostly with students, to design and build beautiful projects often for people of modest means in isolated locations. This, too, had a "both-and" quality as most of them showed artful structures made with activist intentions that built a sense of community.

A sense of community pervaded Ghost 13. The speakers, most of them alumni of previous Ghost Labs, as well as the audience of nearly two hundred architects, educators, critics, and students, displayed a degree of camaraderie that came not only from being together for three days in an isolated location, but also from sharing a common purpose and mission. As Pallasmaa described it, "the best examples of architecture arise from a deep understanding of the place and its climatic and natural characteristics...project[ing] a special beauty, the beauty of human reason and ethics."[7]

Willing Paradise

Creating that beauty in a world torn between the self-indulgent excesses of a few and the undeserved deprivations of so many may seem daunting, but it has not deterred these architects, MacKay-Lyons included. "We have to will paradise into existence," MacKay-Lyons says, "however utopian that may sound." And the Ghost Lab site stands as evidence: an entire landscape conceived and constructed by MacKay-Lyons and his colleagues and students over the last seventeen years, containing everything from a boathouse and barn to cabins and cabanas to houses and horse pastures. "There is aesthetic pleasure in seeing things whole," says MacKay-Lyons, "with designing and making, practice and teaching, family and community as one." The Ghost Lab, he adds, "reminds people that it is possible and that they, too, can live in this way."

MacKay-Lyons sees the small-scale work of the Ghost Lab as relevant to the large-scale problems we face. "Small projects can change the world," he says. "Look at the impact of Glenn Murcutt," who has transformed our thinking about climate-responsive design with a number of modest-size houses. Such aspirations bring to mind CIAM and Team 10—twentieth-century gatherings by a few of the world's leading architects and critics to formulate new directions for architecture and urban design. Unlike those earlier efforts, Ghost 13 did not produce a manifesto or charter (although this book about the conference may serve that role well), but the conference did identify a coherent architectural and educational response to the homogeneity, unsustainability, and inequality of the global economy.

The Importance of Place

That made the location of the conference particularly prescient. When Champlain landed on that Nova Scotia coast a little over four hundred years ago, he—along with the British, who landed in Jamestown a few years later—set in motion the global economy of extracting resources, exploiting native people, and extinguishing species. We tend to see the French and English struggle for power in North America as essentially political and military in nature, but as we look out over the bay where Champlain's ships first set anchor and think about what might have happened differently had his view of the world prevailed, it becomes clear that what mattered in the tension between those two world powers revolved around their differing cultural and environmental agendas.

The French largely had exploration and trade in mind when they established present-day Quebec in 1608, seeking to coexist with the native people. They controlled the number of immigrants allowed to enter New France so as not to overwhelm their few permanent settlements, which they built as compactly and unobtrusively as possible. The same characterized the fur-trading posts the French built on native lands. Constructed of local timber, these posts were inhabited for relatively short periods of time, at which point the traders would burn them to the ground, salvage the nails, and move on, leaving almost no trace behind.

The English took a very different approach. Setting up their first permanent settlement at Jamestown in 1607, the English pursued colonization rather than coexistence, disrupting native populations through military confrontation, land seizure, and the introduction of disease. The English also encouraged settlers to come to the new world, rapidly increasing their numbers and forcing native people and animals to retreat.

The English, of course, not only triumphed over the native populations, but also over the French, who ceded much of their territory after losing the Seven Years' (or French and Indian) War two hundred fifty years ago. This directly affected Nova Scotia, where, during the war, the British deported the French-speaking Acadian population, some of whom returned afterward and many of whom resettled in France or Cajun Louisiana. With the dominance of the commercial, land-owning settlement pattern of the English came the enormous prosperity that many North Americans have since enjoyed, yet also the astounding ecological devastation that we now face.

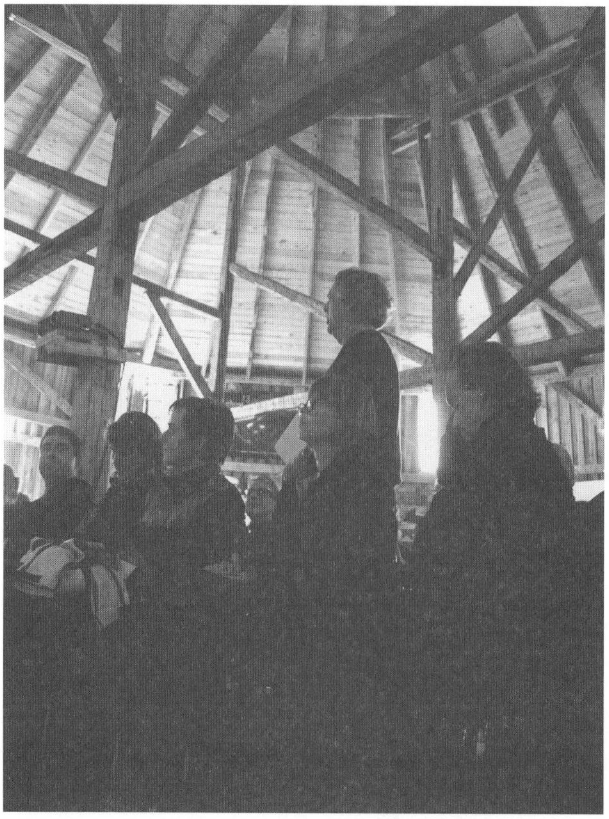

Ghost 13 participants engage in one of the many talks given in the Barn.

While the concept did not yet exist then, the English set about creating what we might now call a "Ponzi scheme" with the continent, exhausting land and resources and taking advantage of other species and people. These practices have brought us to a precipice, in which North Americans now require the equivalent of nearly five Earths to meet our resource requirements and to absorb our waste and pollution.[8] And, like all Ponzi schemes, this one will collapse. We can continue to pretend this won't happen, as most of the investors in Bernard Madoff's Ponzi scheme did until they lost everything, or we can begin to envision life after the global economy, as the Ghost 13 participants have started to do.

Their work shows what living within our ecological footprint might be like. People would live much more modestly, in much closer communities, with much more stewarding of the land and its resources than we do today. Buildings would respond to their climate and culture, constructed by local craftspeople and made of local, renewable, and recyclable materials. And settlements would be more compact, able to sustain themselves largely on what local economies and ecologies can provide.

That may sound unrealistic, but circumstances seem likely to drive us in this direction, whether or not we choose to go. After the fall of the Roman Empire—a fall that Canadian political scientist Thomas Homer-Dixon attributes at least in part to Rome's exhausting the environmental resources on which it depended—Europeans regrouped into small communities that lived locally and sustainably out of necessity.[9] And they rediscovered what the Roman Stoics had long urged upon their over-consuming compatriots: that human beings actually need very little to stay alive, to live well, and to be happy. A good life does not come from having more—more property, more money, more stuff—but from having meaning, which comes from community, collaboration, and coexistence.

What befell the Roman Empire may well happen again, but at a global scale this time and with consequences possibly more dire, given the sheer size of the human population. We can only guess as to what might push us over the edge, whether it would be disruptions of food and water supplies because of climate change or interruptions of fuel and energy resources because of political conflict or eruptions of impoverished or oppressed people because of economic inequalities. However this happens, though, Ghost 13 showed us the role that architects play in this transition. The design community has the ability to envision alternative futures, to help people overcome their fear of change and to see how a healthier, happier, and, as MacKay-Lyons puts it, a "more wholesome existence" can come of it. Located at the place where the global economy began in North America some four hundred years ago, Ghost 13 represented a new kind of beginning for design, one that goes far beyond buildings to ask the question of how we should live if humanity hopes to be here four hundred years from now.

All quotes not otherwise cited come from Brian MacKay-Lyons, in discussion with the author, summer 2011.

1 Brian MacKay-Lyons, *Ghost: Building an Architectural Vision* (New York: Princeton Architectural Press, 2008), 18.

2 Rick Joy, conversation with the audience of Ghost 13, Halifax, Nova Scotia, June 2011.

3 Ghost 13, "Ideas in Things," MacKay-Lyons Sweetapple, Architects, http://mlsarchitects.ca/mobile/ghost.htm.

4 Brian MacKay-Lyons, conversation with the audience of Ghost 13, June 2011.

5 Juhani Pallasmaa, "Architecture and the Human Nature: A Call for a Sustainable Metaphor" (lecture, Ghost 13, June 2011).

6 Ibid.

7 Ibid.

8 Stewart Wallis, "The Four Horsemen of Economics," *The New Economics Foundation Blog*, October 31, 2011. http://www.neweconomics.org/blog/entry/the-four-horsemen-of-economics.

9 Thomas Homer-Dixon, *The Upside of Down: Catastrophe, Creativity and the Renewal of Civilization* (Toronto: Knopf, 2006), 246–50.

KEYNOTES

Critical Regionalism Revisited

Kenneth Frampton

Kenneth Frampton preaches to the choir.

This account of my involvement with the particular mode of beholding known as critical regionalism could perhaps more properly be titled "The Genealogy of Critical Regionalism." As far as I am concerned, the concept dates to 1962, when I became the technical editor of the British magazine *Architectural Design*, a position that I held for just under three years before coming to the United States to teach at Princeton University. Stirling and Gowan had only just completed the Leicester University Engineering Building, and in February 1964 we devoted a considerable number of pages in the magazine to document that work. In the same year, the Economist Building was completed and in 1966 came the swan song of Brutalism, Reyner Banham's book *The New Brutalism*.[1]

These British developments suggest that Brutalism was, in some sense, a regional manifestation, a kind of proto-postmodern sequel to the utopian thrust of the modern movement in its prime. By this I mean the constructivist/purist ethos and the progressive social line that it was broadly associated with prior to the denouement of the Second World War. Around 1963, some eighteen years after the end of the war, during the still enduring postwar, welfare state period—I first felt that a more locally rooted architectural culture could be found in the "city states" of continental Europe than in the equivalent British provincial cities. I began to play with the idea that on the Continent (as we British still referred to it then) and, above all, in the belatedly unified nation-states of Germany, Italy, and the Swiss Federation, one could still identify an intimate connection between the work of a particular architect and the city in which he or she lived and worked. And it was through this all but mythical notion that my coeditor Monica Pidgeon and I began to feature in *Architectural Design* certain architects and works that seemed to be grounded in a particular urban milieu. We brought these connections into focus in the magazine; we published features on such architects as Aris Konstantinidis in Athens, Ernst Gisel in Zurich, Gino Valle in Udine, and Oswald Mathias Ungers in Cologne. We somehow overlooked Carlo Scarpa's particularly fertile connection to Venice, although we published his work, notably his Gavina showroom of 1963. At the time I postulated the notion that there was, in each of these instances, a mutual identification between the architect and the society in which he worked. I thought then, as to some degree I still do, that the way to achieve an authentic, inflected, but still modern architectural culture was to return as a rear guard ploy to grass roots. All of this anticipated the emergence of critical regionalism in the early 1980s. However, the term had yet to be coined.

Toward the end of the 1970s, after a stint on the faculty of the Royal College of Art in London, I found myself back in New York, teaching studio and history/theory at Columbia University alongside Robert Stern. Stern was then riding on the crest of the stylistic postmodern wave; his ideological basis, at the time, embodied Robert Venturi's concept of the "decorated shed" as it had appeared in Venturi's canonical text of 1966, *Complexity and Contradiction in Architecture*.[2] Stern dominated the discourse in the Columbia studios during this period, and I was compelled to recognize that the socioculturally radical modern project in architecture, as in other fields, no longer carried the conviction that it had prior to the tragic outcome of the Spanish Civil War and the ensuing disaster of the Second World War. This, then, was my assessment of the predicament of the postmodern condition in architecture, as I wrote in *Modern Architecture: A Critical History*, the first edition of which appeared in 1980:

> The veil that photo-lithography draws over architecture is not neutral. High-speed photographic and reproductive processes are surely not only the political economy of the sign but also an insidious filter through which our tactile environment tends to lose its concrete responsiveness. When much of modern building is experienced in actuality, its photogenic quality is denied by the poverty and brutality of its detailing. Time and time again an expensive and ostentatious display of either structure or form results in the impoverishment of intimacy; in that which Heidegger has recognized as the loss of "nearness." How rarely do we encounter a modern work where the inflection of a chosen tectonic penetrates into the innermost recesses of the structure, not as a totalizing force but as the declension of an articulate sensibility. That modern society still possesses a capacity for such inflection finds confirmation in the finest work of Aalto.[3]

Also in 1980 Paolo Portoghesi presented a stylistically postmodern architecture exhibition, The End of Prohibition, at the Venice Biennale titled The Presence of the Past. Although I had already declared my veneration for the work of Alvar Aalto as a fundamental ground for a critical modernity, this did not prevent Stern from inviting me to Venice as part of the American delegation to assist with the organization of Portoghesi's Biennale. One visit to Venice was enough for me, however. I promptly resigned once I understood where "the end of prohibition" was going to end up: that is, in the false fronts of the Strada Novissima built by the operatives of *Cinecittà*, designed by a spectrum of architects ranging from Stern to Arata Isozaki, Rem Koolhaas to Leon Krier—Krier being the only one to insist that his false front be made of real materials.

The Venice Biennale experience stimulated, as a reaction, my 1983 essay "Towards a Critical Regionalism," which first appeared in Hal Foster's anthology, *The Anti-Aesthetic: Essays on Postmodern Culture*.[4] Also influencing my essay was a critical response to *Modern Architecture: A Critical History*. *Architectural Design* had published a design profile on the book with commissioned reviews by leading architects and critics, including Alan Colquhoun, David Dunster, Rafael Moneo, Alberto Pérez-Gómez, Demetri Porphyrios, Manfredo Tafuri, and Bruno Zevi. All of those invited agreed to write something with the exception of the Czech émigré, architect, and phenomenologist Dalibor Vesely, who was then teaching in the school of architecture at Cambridge. To my chagrin, Vesely refused, saying that what I had tried to elucidate in my final chapter had been handled much more succinctly and profoundly by the French philosopher Paul Ricoeur in a 1961 essay titled "Universal Civilization and National Cultures."[5] I immediately sought out this text, which oriented me toward what would soon become the philosophical basis of my regionalist argument. This finally came to light in "Towards a Critical Regionalism."

Ricoeur's evocation of the time-honored distinction between civilization and culture had a decisive and lasting impact on my way of looking at the world, so much so that I cannot forgo quoting his words here. Despite the slightly dated tone, his appraisal of the predicament of modernization is still as pertinent now as it was half a century ago, when France was in the throes of divesting itself of its last colony:

> The phenomenon of universalization, while being an advancement of mankind, at the same time constitutes a sort of subtle destruction, not only of traditional cultures, which might not be an irreparable wrong, but also of what I shall call for the time being the creative nucleus of great civilizations and great cultures, that nucleus on the basis of which we interpret life, what I shall call in advance the ethical and mythical nucleus of mankind. The conflict springs up from there. We have the feeling that this single world civilization at the same time exerts a sort of attrition or wearing away at the expense of the cultural resources which have made the great civilizations of the past. This threat is expressed, among other disturbing effects, by the spreading before our eyes of a mediocre civilization which is the absurd counterpart of what I was just calling elementary culture. Everywhere throughout the world, one finds the same bad movie, the same slot machines, the same plastic or aluminum atrocities, the same twisting of language by propaganda, etc. It seems as if mankind, by approaching *en masse* a basic consumer culture, were also stopped *en masse* at a subcultural level. Thus we come to the crucial problem confronting nations just rising from underdevelopment. In order to get onto the road toward modernization, is it necessary to jettison the old cultural past which has been the *raison d'être* of a nation?...Whence the paradox: on the

> one hand, it has to root itself in the soil of its past, forge a national spirit, and unfurl this spiritual and cultural revindication before the colonialist's personality. But in order to take part in modern civilization, it is necessary at the same time to take part in scientific, technical, and political rationality, something which very often requires the pure and simple abandon of a whole cultural past. It is a fact: every culture cannot sustain and absorb the shock of modern civilization. There is the paradox: how to become modern and to return to sources; how to revive an old, dormant civilization and take part in universal civilization.[6]

In "Towards a Critical Regionalism," I followed Ricoeur's words with my "Six Points for an Architecture of Resistance," which included culture and civilization; the rise and fall of the avant-garde; critical regionalism and world culture; the resistance of the place-form; culture vs. nature topography: context, climate, light, and tectonic form; and visual versus tactile.

My advocacy of a resistant cultural strategy was directly indebted (as I made clear through my citation of their work) to Alexander Tzonis and Liane Lefaivre's canonical essay of 1981, "The Grid and the Pathway," in which they coined the term "Critical Regionalism." In their essay, they compared the topographic rationalism of Aris Konstantinidis's "grid" to the organic topography of Dimitris Pikionis's "pathway" in the paved, rubble-stone staging ground built on Philopappos Hill outside the Acropolis in Athens in 1959. From this comparison, Tzonis and Lefaivre made the first pertinent formulation of critical regionalism:

> Regionalism has dominated architecture in almost all countries at some time during the past two centuries and a half. By way of general definition, we can say that it upholds the individual and local architectonic features against more universal and abstract ones. In addition, however, regionalism bears the hallmark of ambiguity. On the one hand, it has been associated with movements of reform and liberation...on the other, it has proved a powerful tool of repression and chauvinism....Certainly, critical regionalism has its limitations. The upheaval of the populist movement—a more developed form of regionalism—has brought to light these weak points. No new architecture can emerge without a new kind of relations between designer and user, without new kinds of programs....Despite these limitations critical regionalism is a bridge over which any humanistic architecture of the future must pass.[7]

A number of critiques and countercritiques of this thesis have appeared over the past thirty years, including my own 1990 essay "Rappel à l'ordre: The Case for the Tectonic," in which I distanced myself somewhat from this view.[8] In my 1995 book, *Studies in Tectonic Culture: The Poetics of Construction in Nineteenth and Twentieth Century Architecture*, I tried to reground some kind of resistant argument in what I had the temerity to call "the poetics of construction."[9] Then came a brilliantly sympathetic critique of my thesis by someone who was totally outside the field of architecture, the Marxist literary critic Fredric Jameson, whose book *The Seeds of Time* presented, among other things, the following judgment on the cultural/political limitations of critical regionalism. In his brilliant counterthesis, Jameson returned to the idea of the decorated shed.

> Frampton's conceptual proposal, however, is not an internal but rather geopolitical one: it seeks to mobilize a pluralism of "regional" styles (a term selected, no doubt, in order to forestall the unwanted connotations of the terms national and international alike), with a view toward resisting the standardizations of a henceforth global late capitalism and corporation, whose "vernacular" is as omnipresent as its power over local decisions (and indeed, after the end of the Cold War, over local governments and individual nation states as well).
>
> It is thus politically important, returning to the problem of parts or components, to emphasize the degree to which the concept of Critical Regionalism is necessarily allegorical. What the individual buildings are henceforth here a unit of is no longer a unique vision of city planning (such as the Baroque) nor a specific city fabric (like Las Vegas) but rather a distinctive regional culture as a whole, for which the distinctive individual building becomes a metonym. The construction of such a building resembles the two previously discussed movements of a stylistic postmodernism and Italian Neorationalism to the degree to which it must also deploy a storehouse of preexisting forms and traditional motifs, as signs and markers by which to "decorate" what generally remains a relatively conventional Western "shed."[10]

In their 2003 book *Critical Regionalism: Architecture and Identity in a Globalized World*, Lefaivre and Tzonis categorically dismissed my Critical Regionalist position as chauvinistic.[11] What they no doubt meant by this, although they did not spell it out, is that it was too regressively Heideggerian. Many other criticisms followed, notably those in Vincent B. Canizaro's 2007 reader, *Architectural Regionalism: Collected Writings on Place, Identity, Modernity, and Tradition*.[12] Of the many critiques in that book, none is perhaps as inadvertently prejudicial as Keith Eggener's "Placing Resistance: A Critique of Critical Regionalism," wherein he cites Marina Waismann to the effect that "the Latin American version of regionalism is quite different from that proposed by Kenneth Frampton or Alex Tzonis and Liane Lefaivre...and that it should be properly understood as a *divergence* rather than a *resistance*."[13] Both Eggener and Waismann tended to regard critical regionalism as a superimposition of concepts originating in the center rather than on the periphery. Although I never categorically stated as much, I feel that this mode of beholding is as pertinent to the center as to the periphery, inasmuch as the juggernaut of civilization in the form of maximizing technology is a threat at a time when the difference between center and periphery is less and less relevant, and when the consumerist tendency to commodify everything, everywhere, continues unabated. For example, the traditional urban fabric of London is being as relentlessly destroyed by freestanding, commodifying high-rise buildings as, say, the traditional urban fabric of Kurashiki in Japan, which after the Second World War was still intact.

In 1986 in my reformulation of critical regionalism in the second edition of *Modern Architecture: A Critical History*, I allowed the voices of the periphery to speak for themselves.[14] I cited Álvaro Siza Vieira for his Beires House in Portugal (1976) and for the importance he gave to the idea of transformation, anticipating his ironic slogan: "Architects don't invent anything, they just transform reality." Elsewhere I quoted Luis Barragán for the memories of his childhood in the Mexican village of Mazamitla, which he recalled with the words, "No, I have no photographs, I have only the memory," and Harwell Hamilton Harris for his distinction between regionalisms:[15]

> Opposed to the Regionalism of Restriction is another type of regionalism: the Regionalism of Liberation. This is the manifestation of a region that is especially in tune with the emerging thought of the time. We call such a manifestation "regional" only because it has not yet emerged elsewhere. It is the genius of this region to be more than ordinarily aware and more than ordinarily free. Its virtue is that its manifestation has significance of the world outside itself. To express this regionalism architecturally it is necessary that there be building—preferably a lot of building—at one time. Only so can the expression be sufficiently general, sufficiently varied, sufficiently forceful to capture people's imaginations and provide a friendly climate long enough for a new school of design to develop.[16]

Three years after writing "Towards a Critical Regionalism," I began to move away from this position largely because whenever I lectured on the subject in the United States I was met with the objection, particularly by students, that there were no roots of a regional culture or identity remaining in their particular location, despite the evident variations in climate, geology, etc. I thought to myself then, as I do now, that this was to some extent the consequence of universal air-conditioning as a maximized technology. In any event, I moved away from this allegorical theme to focus not on technology as an end in itself as per the British high-tech movement, but rather on the tectonic as a "poetic of construction." I based my four Cullinan Lectures at Rice University in Texas in 1986 on the architects Auguste Perret, Mies van der Rohe, Louis Kahn, and Jørn Utzon; the lectures formed the core of Studies in Tectonic Culture. As noted earlier, my writings informed Jameson's critique of critical regionalism in *The Seeds of Time*, in which he wrote:

> In fact, however, Frampton has a more formal alternative to these particular aesthetic modes—an alternative framed by the tripartite values of the tactile, the tectonic, and the telluric, which frame the notion of space in such a way that it turns back slowly into a conception of place once again. This alternative tends now to displace those parts of the building that are visible (and thus lend themselves to categories of the visual arts) in favor of a "privileging of the joint as the primordial tectonic element"; a nonvisual and nonrepresentational category which Frampton attributes to Gottfried Semper and which for him constitutes "the fundamental nexus around which building comes into being, that is to say, comes to be articulated as a presence in itself." The category of the joint as a primal articulation of the two forces that meet in it (along with its correlative of the "'break' or 'dis-joint'...that point at which things break against each other rather than connect: that significant fulcrum at which one system, surface or material abruptly ends to give way to another") would seem to be the fundamental innovation of the aesthetic of Critical Regionalism, whose non- or anti-representational equivalent for the other arts (or literature) remains to be worked out.[17]

After four decades of involvement with critical regionalism, where do I stand now with regard to the predicament of architecture in an increasingly globalized world? One possible response is to focus on the finite capacity of the earth to sustain the regeneration of the human species as a whole. In the latest edition of *Modern Architecture: A Critical History*, I discussed the last twenty years of pluralist production under the rubric of the following six categories: Topography, Morphology, Sustainability, Materiality, Habitat, and Civic Form.[18] These categories were discussed under a gloss drawn from a seminar held in New Zealand and published under the title, *Is Capitalism Sustainable?: Political Economy and the Politics of Ecology.* The gloss came from Martin O'Connor's contribution to the seminar, in which he stated:

> The globalization of capital is, of course, somewhat spurious. Yet it is an important ideological innovation. The capitalist system undergoes a kind of mutation to its essential form, the culmination of which would be the complete (notional) capitalization of nature in which there no longer remains any domain external to capital. This is tantamount to the assumption that an external nature does not exist. The image is no longer Marx's (or the classical economists') of human beings acting on external nature to produce value. Rather, the image is of the diverse elements of nature (including human nature) themselves codified as capital. Nature is capital, or, rather, nature is conceived in the image of capital. The logic of the system is thus the subsumption of all the elements of nature-considered-as-capital to the finality of capital's expanded reproduction.
>
> Theoretical difficulties immediately arise as a result of the fact that this is a largely imaginary functional integration the rhetoric stresses harmonization and optimization; the reality is disorder and conflict. As Baudrillard remarks, "Everything is potentially functional and nothing is in fact." Two sources of contradiction are inherent in the process of the capitalization of nature, which furnish our justifications for proposing a shift from an industrial to an ecological Marxist perspective on production, on the "eventual" and "inevitable" collapse of capitalism, and thence on the conditions for some sort of socialism. The first is the fact that the planet is materially finite, a situation that creates biophysical limits to the accumulation process. The second, which is synergetic with the first, is the fact that capital does not and cannot control the reproduction and modification of the "natural" conditions of production in the same way it purposes to regulate industrial commodity production.[19]

In many respects such an overriding "ecopolitical" critique brings one back to the possibility of critical regionalism as a kind of one-off, quixotic site of resistance. While it is not able to alter the dominant spectacular, technoscientific global corporate discourse, it is nonetheless still able to articulate a resistant *place-form* within a smaller society, which, here and there, may maintain a dissenting cultural and political position.

1 Reyner Banham, *The New Brutalism* (London: Architectural Press, 1966).

2 Robert Venturi, *Complexity and Contradiction in Architecture* (New York: Museum of Modern Art Press, 1966).

3 Kenneth Frampton, *Modern Architecture: A Critical History*, 4th ed. (London: Thames & Hudson, 2007), 343.

4 Hal Foster, ed., *The Anti-Aesthetic: Essays on Postmodern Culture* (Port Townsend, WA: Bay Press, 1983).

5 Paul Ricoeur, "Universalization and National Cultures," in *History and Truth* (Evanston, IL: Northwestern University Press, 1961), 276–83.

6 Ibid., 276–77.

7 Alexander Tzonis and Liane Lefaivre, "The Grid and the Pathway," *Architecture in Greece* 15 (1981): 178.

8 Kenneth Frampton, "Rappel à l'ordre: The Case for the Tectonic," *Architectural Design* 60, no. 3–4 (1990): 19–25.

9 Kenneth Frampton, *Studies in Tectonic Culture: The Poetics of Construction in Nineteenth and Twentieth Century Architecture*, ed. John Cava (Cambridge, MA: MIT Press, 1995).

10 Fredric Jameson, *The Seeds of Time* (New York: Columbia University Press, 1996), 202–3.

11 Liane Lefaivre and Alexander Tzonis, *Critical Regionalism: Architecture and Identity in a Globalized World* (Munich and London: Prestel, 2003).

12 Vincent B. Canizaro, ed., *Architectural Regionalism: Collected Writings on Place, Identity, Modernity, and Tradition* (New York: Princeton Architectural Press, 2007).

13 Keith Eggener, "Placing Resistance: A Critique of Critical Regionalism," in Canizaro, 204.

14 Kenneth Frampton, *Modern Architecture: A Critical History*, 2nd ed. (London: Thames & Hudson, 1986), last chapter.

15 Emilio Ambasz, *The Architecture of Luis Barragan* (New York: Museum of Modern Art, 1976).

16 Harwell Hamilton Harris, "Regionalism and Nationalism" (address to the Northwest Regional Council of the AIA, Eugene, Oregon, 1954).

17 Jameson, *The Seeds of Time*, 197.

18 Frampton, *Modern Architecture*, 4th ed., Part 3, Chapter 7.

19 Martin O'Connor, "Codependency and Indeterminacy: A Critique of the Theory of Production," in *Is Capitalism Sustainable?: Political Economy and the Politics of Ecology* (New York & London: Guilford Press, 1994), 55.

Architecture and Human Nature: A Call for a Sustainable Metaphor

Juhani Pallasmaa

Juhani Pallasmaa speaks about sustainable metaphors.

My work always tried to unite the true with the beautiful; but when I had to choose one or the other, I usually chose the beautiful.
—Hermann Weyl[1]

The call for an ecological ethics, lifestyle, and mindset of sustainability is surely the most important force of change in the field of architecture since the breakthrough of modernity a century ago. Architectural history is seen as a succession of varying stylistic canons, but today's challenge calls for a new understanding of the very essence of architecture. We continue to see ourselves and our artifacts as independent of nature, but the challenge of today is also likely to alter the received polarity between nature and the human artifact. I have elsewhere described this paradigmatic change as the shift from metaphorical functionalism to ecological functionalism.[2] This challenge calls for a new understanding of goals and processes, aesthetics and performance, form and function, rationality and beauty, artistic objectives and ethics, and, finally, of ourselves as children of Mother Earth.

The Machine Metaphor

Functionalist thinking has regarded functional and technical performance mainly in terms of the aestheticized mechanical metaphor. The mechanized object even became an ideal in the arts: "The object has to become the main character of modern painting and it has to throw the human figure from the throne. If the person, the face or the body turn into objects, a great freedom opens up to the modern artist...to me the human face or figure does not have more meaning than a bunch of keys or a bicycle," wrote Fernand Léger.[3] Ever since that era, architecture has been dealt with primarily in terms of problem solving, functional equations, and the design of aestheticized metaphoric machines, as exemplified by Le Corbusier's influential credo of 1923, "A house is a machine to live in."[4]

Today's ecological imperative calls for an architecture whose performance is credibly identifiable and measurable, not just metaphoric or symbolic. This requirement suggests a nonautonomous architecture that becomes part of natural processes and cycles. Yet visual dominance in architecture continues to prevail. In fact, the purely visual understanding of the art of architecture may never have been more dominant than in today's architecture of the commercialized image, reinforced by digital media and worldwide journalism. Even sustainability is most often judged by the eye as an aesthetic and symbolic aspiration rather than through an analysis of actual performance. In the age of ecology, the concept of "form" has to be seen as a temporal process or emergent situation, rather than a closed and finite aesthetic entity.

False Sustainability

During the past decade, images of "sustainability" have become symbolic of progressive and responsible design, and various technical devices are frequently added onto rather conservative projects to create the desired progressive image. Sustainable design has also become a new marketing strategy both among designers and developers. Regrettably, the established methods of evaluating sustainable qualities of design tend to support this superficial view, rather than stimulate profoundly valid ecological thinking, lifestyle, and ethics. This opportunistic way of using "sustainable" design as a shrewd means of commercial manipulation hides the real issues. The emotionally and ethically appealing concept of sustainability can even undermine true sustainability, as it makes us believe that we are already doing our share in this big task. By designing a LEED-certified building, we justify not only the continuation of our suicidal economic ideology, but also its continued acceleration.

The true criterion of sustainability implies the evaluation of projects as entire processes: harvesting and producing the materials; the processes of manufacture, transportation, and construction; use and maintenance; and eventual dismantling and demolition of the structure. Equally important are the reuse of materials and components, and analysis of the overall material and energy consumption, as well as the toxic and otherwise harmful side effects and products. The processes have to be analyzed and evaluated in relation to the continuum of time, not merely through the momentary judgment of the aesthetic eye or short-term balance sheet. As the entire life cycle is added to the already complex logistical equation of architecture, nobody seems to be able to grasp the entirety with scientific certainty.

Architecture: An Impure Discipline

I have called architecture an "impure" and "messy" discipline because it contains inherently irreconcilable ingredients, such as metaphysical, cultural, and economic aspirations; functional, technical, and aesthetic objectives, etc. In fact, I cannot think of a more complex human activity or artifact than architecture. The conflicting aspirations that are an inseparable part of human architecture tend to turn our constructions toward irrationality. The great Norwegian architect Sverre Fehn once said to me: "The bird's nest is absolute functionalism because the bird is not conscious of its death."[5] Our human actions, however, are deeply motivated by our suppressed fear of death. To condense the "illogical" nature of architecture, we can say that architecture is at the same time the means and the end.

As Alvar Aalto claimed in the 1950s, only artistic vision can bring the thousands of conflicting ingredients in an architectural problem into a harmonious synthesis.[6] Yet, from the perspective of sustainability, the various crucial qualities of this synthesis have to pass critical evaluation and measurement. I am not preaching of a "scientific architecture"; I suggest an architecture that is grounded in the full existential understanding of human destiny, and this view certainly calls for a deeply lived vision more than scientific formulations. Our task is more ethical than technical. Architecture is not only engaged with today, it also expresses what we want to become tomorrow. We build and dwell in accordance with our thoughts, fears, and dreams.

The Lived Metaphor

We architects are used to thinking in terms of space and material form; we think of objects rather than systems, aesthetics rather than processes, visual qualities rather than existential issues, and the present rather than the temporal continuum. As philosophers George Lakoff and Mark Johnson have convincingly shown in their book *The Metaphors We Live By* (1980), language, thought, and action are metaphorical: "Metaphor is pervasive in everyday life, not just in language but in thought and action. Our ordinary conceptual systems, in terms of which we both think and act, are fundamentally metaphorical in nature," the authors claim.[7] Psychiatrist Arnold H. Modell argues similarly that we are not even aware of the metaphors that guide our thought: "Metaphor is primarily a form of cognition rather than a trope or figure of speech. Further, metaphor as a cognitive tool can operate unconsciously, so that a metaphoric process is one aspect of the unconscious mind."[8] This psychiatrist-philosopher suggests that we are guided by our own metaphors as much as we consciously mold them. Indeed, Aristotle acknowledged in his *Poetics*: "The greatest thing by far is to be master of metaphor, [which is] the one thing that cannot be learned from others, and it is also a sign of genius."[9] Along with metaphor, analogy and synecdoche are our essential tools of thought. Like verbal and poetic thinking, architectural thinking is engaged in metaphors and analogues. In fact, we can think of buildings as material, embodied, and lived metaphors.

Architecture and Image of Self

We live in metaphors. Buildings, structures, and cities are constructed material images of our view of the world, belief systems, and fears, as well as of ourselves, as much as they are practical devices. The interplay or, better, total fusion of the mental and material dimensions of life is usually disregarded when thinking of architecture. We tend to forget that every human construction, beautiful or ugly, reasonable or outrageous, always originates in the human mind. One of my personal missions as an architectural writer has been to emphasize the total interpenetration of these two worlds. In the words of Robert Pogue Harrison: "In the fusion of place and soul, the soul is as much a container of place as place is a container of soul, and both are susceptible to the same forces of destruction."[10] When building structures of concrete and steel, we also build immaterial and imaginary structures of ideas, percepts, and ideals. The essential task of architecture is to improve the world that we live in, to make it a better place for ourselves to be in. As Rainer Maria Rilke beautifully writes: "Art is not a little selective sample of the world, it is a transformation of the world, an endless transformation towards the good."[11] In his inspiring book on Venice, *Watermark*, the Nobel Laureate poet Joseph Brodsky states: "In the end, like the Almighty Himself, we make everything in our image, for want of a more reliable model; our artifacts tell more about ourselves than our confessions."[12]

The Changing Metaphor

The guiding metaphors of building have shifted, historically, from images of shelter to mechanistic images to today's electric, electronic, and digital models of invisible performance. Tomorrow, we may turn to the staggering complexity and precision of biological phenomena. Edward O. Wilson, the biologist, defines the new attitude of biophilia "as the innate tendency to focus on life and lifelike processes."[13] The currently prevailing globalized architecture of alluring and memorable images usually flattens architecture into three-dimensional pictures—spatial advertisements, as it were. It is evident that the new Brave Digital World, to paraphrase the title of Aldous Huxley's gloomy book, has so far facilitated questionable processes of globalization more than it has genuinely helped the cause of architecture.[14] I venture to say that the computer has been largely misused from the ethical point of view to advance instant and fluid commerce and control the world over.

It is most likely that the future models and metaphors of thought and design, from everyday technology to computer and material sciences, and from economics and medicine to architecture, will increasingly be based on biological imagery—not biomorphic forms, but the often incredible subtlety and complexity of biological systems of interaction, dynamic balance, and emergence. This approach, inspired by models of biological performance, has already emerged in such areas of investigation as bionics and biomimicry. The single argument by Wilson, the world's leading myrmecologist and spokesman for biophilic ethics, to the effect that the "superorganism" of the leaf-cutter ant's nest alone is a more complex system in its performance than any human invention and is unimaginably old, should convince anyone that the biological world offers exciting models for the refinement of human artifacts and systems.[15] Indeed, complex traffic systems are today designed based on the traffic systems of ants, and self-cleaning glass and numerous other inventions have been made through the study of biological precedents. New revolutionary carbon computers are also being developed based on the computing principles of our own neural nets.

Animal Architecture: Lessons for Architectural Craft

Permit me to say firmly: I do not support any romantic biomorphic architecture. I advocate an architecture that arises from respect for nature in its complexity, not only its visual characteristics, and from empathy and loyalty to all forms of life and from a humility about our own destiny.

Indeed, architecture cannot regress; all life forms and strategies of nature keep developing and refining. The magnitude of our problems calls for extremely refined, responsive, and subtle technologies. That is the kind of technology nature uses, from the smallest parts to the most complex entities. Nature uses self-repairing materials, such as the rhinoceros' horn, which is not live tissue yet repairs its wounds, and the inner shell of the abalone, which is twice as tough as high-tech ceramics and deforms under stress like a metal, instead of breaking.

I have myself been interested in animal constructions since my early childhood at my grandfather's humble farm in Finland during the war years, and the more I have studied this subject matter the more amazed I am. Many readers are surely familiar with the fact that the dragline of the spider is the toughest material yet known; its tensile strength is more than three times that of steel. Spider silk consists of small crystallites embedded in a rubbery matrix of organic polymer—a composite material that evolved tens of millions of years before our current age of composite materials. The spider silk line is even tougher than polyaramid Kevlar, the material used for bulletproof vests and facial masks for riot police. Significantly, the spider produces its line at body temperature with no poisonous side products, whereas Kevlar is produced in pressurized vats with concentrated sulphuric acid at very high temperatures, in a process that creates problematic toxic by-products.[16] Readers may also know that the African termite Macrotermes bellicosus seems to be able to choose between two theories of physics in the construction of the collective artificial lung in its nest community of ten million inhabitants, depending on whether they happen to live in the moist coastal areas or arid central regions of Africa.[17]

It is becoming evident that we have distanced ourselves too far from nature, with grave consequences. The research of the Finnish allergologist Tari Haahtela has shown convincingly that many of the so-called civilization diseases, such as allergies, diabetes, depression, many types of cancer, and even obesity, are consequences of living in environments that are too sterile and "artificial." We have destroyed the natural bacterial habitats in our intestines. This specialist in allergies tells us that he has never met an allergy patient "with earth under his fingernails."[18]

The Prevailing View of Man

I believe that the view of ourselves that prevails in Western thinking, daily practices, and education has to be fundamentally reevaluated. Wilson argues: "All of man's troubles may well arise…from the fact that we do not know what we are and do not agree on what we want to become."[19] We first need to give up the hubris of regarding ourselves as the center of the universe, and as the Homo sapiens, the species that knows. We should also stop seeing ourselves as the image of God. We are not the image of God; the grand systems of the universe and nature are.

Without going too far into philosophical and ethical judgment as well as recent scientific thought, I want to mention some aspects of our own humanity that need to be reconsidered. These suggestions have direct implications for architecture.

A New View of Humanity

Firstly, we need to accept the essentially embodied essence of human existence, experience, cognition, and memory. As Maurice Merleau-Ponty writes, "The painter takes his body with him, says [Paul] Valery. Indeed, we cannot imagine how a mind could paint."[20] We can say the same about architects; architecture is constituted in our embodied way of being in the world, and it articulates that very mode of being. Besides, buildings unconsciously represent the body.

Secondly, we are fundamentally sensory and sensual beings. Architecture is possibly engaged with a dozen different but integrated sensory systems, not just the five Aristotelian senses. Steinerian philosophy, in fact, identifies twelve senses.[21] The senses especially central in architecture are the existential sense, the sense of self, and the sense of temporal continuum and causality.

Thirdly, perception, thinking, and memorizing are complex activities that are fundamentally based on embodied processes and mental or neural images, rather than words and language. Language is a secondary articulation of these neural patterns. The language of architecture is primarily a nonconscious embodied and existential dialogue. This is where the logocentric theories of architecture go astray. Colin St. John Wilson writes about this archaic and existential language:

> It is as if I am being manipulated by some subliminal code, not to be translated into words, which acts directly on the nervous system and imagination, at the same time stirring intimations of meaning with vivid spatial experience as though they were one thing. It is my belief that the code acts so directly and vividly upon us because it is strangely familiar, it is in fact the first language we ever learned, long before words, and which is now recalled to us through art, which alone holds the key to revive it.[22]

Fourthly, human intelligence is routinely described by IQ, but this is a very crude and uninformed view of intelligence. In accordance with psychologist Howard Gardner's current studies, there are ten categories of human intelligence. He first lists seven categories of intelligence: linguistic, logical-mathematical, musical, bodily-kinesthetic, spatial, interpersonal, and intrapersonal. Later, he suggests three more categories: naturalistic, spiritual, and existential intelligence.[23] I would add the categories of emotional, aesthetic, and ethical intelligence to the list of human cognitive capacities. Emotional intelligence, in fact, could well be the most instant, synthetic, holistic, integrated, and reliable of our systems of reacting to complex environmental and social situations. By emotions, we judge complex life situations, such as the ambience, mood, or atmosphere of a space, or place, whereas the scope of IQ intelligence is limited. Mood may well be the most synthetic of architectural features, but it has hardly been consciously analyzed or theorized. Indeed, as architects, we need to sharpen at least twelve categories of sensing and the same number of modes of intelligence in order to do our job well.

The Marvelous Brain

We tend to think of our behavior in terms of our conscious faculties, but consciousness accounts for only a tiny fraction of the ways in which we relate to the world. According to Matti Bergström, a Finnish neurologist, the information capacity of a single nerve fiber, and also of our consciousness, is about one hundred bits per second. On the basis of the human brain's synapses, he calculates that the information-handling capacity of our entire brain is in the category of ten to the seventeenth degree.[24] This dizzying figure helps to explain why our surroundings can have a dramatically stronger impact on us than we can consciously identify and analyze, not to speak of being able to describe these interdependences verbally.[25] As I said earlier, we have great capacity to decipher atmospheres or ambiences, which are very complex environmental situations.

Recent research in neurobiology promises a new understanding of our own brain activities in general, and more particularly the meaning of aesthetic judgment and pleasure. In his pioneering book *Inner Vision: An Exploration of Art and the Brain*, neurologist Semir Zeki suggests the possibility "of a theory of aesthetics that is biologically based."[26] I personally have no doubt about it; what else could beauty be than one of nature's powerful instruments of selection? A culture that is losing its sense of beauty is already declining. Zeki also argues that "art [is] an extension of the functions of the visual brain in its search for essentials."[27] No doubt, architecture is similarly an extension of our neural system to facilitate our constant search for meaning and a satisfactory relationship with the world. Architectural structures decisively increase the order and predictability of the environment.

"Most painters are also neurologists...they are those who have experimented upon and, without ever realising it, understood something about the organization of the visual brain, though with techniques that are unique to them," Zeki writes.[28] We can undoubtedly make the same assumption about profound architects. They grasp the essence of human nature in addition to being sensitive to the characteristics of space and form. Great architects are able to create atmospheres that make us feel safe and comfortable. As Gaston Bachelard suggests, "The chief benefit of the house [is that it] shelters daydreaming, the house protects the dreamer, the house allows one to dream in peace."[29]

Architectural Time

Modern architecture has been largely future oriented. Yet we are primarily historical and biological beings whose neural systems, senses, and reactions have developed over millions of years. Time in biology has different scales than in human culture, such as organismic time, biochemical time, ecological time, and evolutionary time. Architecture deals with the dimensions of time as essentially as with space. "Architecture is not only about domesticating space, it is also a deep defence against the terror of time. The language of beauty is essentially the language of timeless reality," Karsten Harries, the philosopher, writes.[30] Architecture articulates our experience of time and the historical dimension, and it also reconnects us with our past.

The modernist poet Ezra Pound argues that the arts need to maintain their umbilical cord to their own archaic origins: "Music begins to atrophy when it departs too far from the dance...poetry begins to atrophy when it gets too far from music."[31] I wish to add that, in my view, architecture withers when it departs too far from the primary experiences and images of dwelling.

Along with the inspiration brought about by biological models, a deeper understanding of our own biological and cultural historicity is needed. We have the tailbone as a reminder of our arboreal life, the remains of a horizontal plica semilunaris of our saurian phase, and traces of gills from our fish life, and we must have similar mental remnants in our collective memory. In fact, Freud assumed the existence of "archaic remnants" as he theorized the unconscious human mind. The origins of architectural pleasure, such as the opposite notions of 'prospect' and 'refuge,' or the pleasure of open fire, can similarly be traced back to our evolutionary history. To head enthusiastically into a digital, computer-generated virtual world, forgetting where we have come from, seems careless to me. I see the defense of our biological and historical essence and of the authenticity and autonomy of experience as crucial tasks of art and architecture. A "mental ecology" is needed to expand the notion of ecology into the human mental world, as ecology and sustainability cannot be dealt with merely in technical terms.

The Ideology of Suicide

It is shocking to notice that during the recent worldwide recessions, no major political figure or economic expert has touched upon the obsessive ideal of perpetual growth, which undoubtedly is the basic cause of our escalating environmental—and I would say also our social—problems. The unanimous concern worldwide has been to get the wheels running again, at least at the same pace as before the financial collapse. Unless we face the real issues related to our biased beliefs and objectives, no sustainable architecture can decisively change the suicidal course of industrial civilizations. Shouldn't we follow the example of social insects who have happily refined their constructions during tens or hundreds of millions of years and who will undoubtedly continue to do so after the human species is gone?

City planning, construction of infrastructures, and architecture form the core concern in orienting human destiny toward a sustainable and more dignified future. Gardening and landscape architecture already provide models for a softer, fragile, and time-conscious design practice. Ethical changes in thought and values are bound to arise from individuals, as societies do not seem to be capable of learning. As architects, the wise development of a sustainable attitude to life is our ethical share in this enormous task. In today's consumer culture, architecture is mostly seen as the design and production of aestheticized commodities. I wish to argue firmly that architecture is too deeply biologically, culturally, existentially, and mentally grounded in our historicity—and I am here referring primarily to our biohistoricity—to be merely a realm of aesthetics or commerce. Or, rather, even our aesthetic desire and longing for beauty have to be seen in an existential and biological perspective, not as mere pleasure or marketing strategy.

As Brodsky argues, "Man is an aesthetic being before becoming an ethical being."[32] Sustainable architecture has a future only if we can make it aesthetically exciting and seductive. Paradoxically, sustainability has to be turned into a new concept of beauty. For me, the best examples of architecture that arise from a deep understanding of place and its climatic and natural characteristics—such as Glenn Murcutt's buildings and the humane high-tech buildings by Renzo Piano, which exploit refined construction methods and new material technologies for the purposes of dynamic energy efficiency—project a special beauty, the beauty of human reason and ethics. Brodsky assures us with the conviction of a poet: "Believe it or not, the purpose of evolution is beauty."[33]

1 As quoted in Edward O. Wilson, *Biophilia: The Human Bond with Other Species* (Cambridge, MA: Harvard University Press, 1984), 61. Weyl, a mathematician, perfected quantum and relativity theory.

2 Juhani Pallasmaa, "From Metaphorical to Ecological Functionalism," in Juhani Pallasmaa, *Encounters: Architectural Essays*, ed. Peter MacKeith (Helsinki: Rakennustieto Publishing, 2005), 177–89.

3 Fernand Léger, *Maalaustaiteen tehtävät* [The tasks of painting] (Jyväskylä, Finland: K. J. Gummerus, 1981), 63, 69.

4 Le Corbusier, *Towards a New Architecture* (London: The Architectural Press, 1959), 89.

5 Sverre Fehn, conversation with the author in the Villa Mairea, 1985.

6 Alvar Aalto, "Art and Technology" (1955), in *Alvar Aalto in His Own Words*, ed. Göran Schildt (Helsinki: Otava Publishing Company, 1997), 174.

7 George Lakoff and Mark Johnson, *Metaphors We Live By* (Chicago: University of Chicago Press, 1980), 3.

8 Arnold H. Modell, *Imagination and the Meaningful Brain* (Cambridge, MA: MIT Press, 2006), xii.

9 Aristotle, *Poetics* 59a 8–10, as quoted in Arthur C. Danto, *Beyond the Brillo Box: The Visual Arts in Post-Historical Perspective* (New York: Farrar, Straus & Giroux, 1992), 73.

10 Robert Pogue Harrison, "Sympathetic Miracles," in *Gardens: An Essay on the Human Condition* (Chicago: University of Chicago Press, 2008), 130.

11 Rainer Maria Rilke, letter to Jakob von Uexküll, Paris, August 19, 1909, "Lukijalle" [To the reader], Rainer Maria Rilke, *Hiljainen taiteen sisin: kirjeitä vuosilta 1900–1926* [The silent innermost core of art; letters 1900–1926], ed. Liisa Enwald (Helsinki: TAI-teos, 1997), 8.

12 Joseph Brodsky, *Watermark* (London and New York: Penguin Books, 1992), 61.

13 Wilson, *Biophilia*, 1.

14 Aldous Huxley, *Brave New World* (1932; repr., New York: Harper Perennial Modern Classics, 2006).

15 Wilson, *Biophilia*, 37.

16 Janine M. Benyus, *Biomimicry: Invention Inspired by Nature* (New York: Quill William Morrow, 1997), 132.

17 Karl von Frisch, *Animal Architecture* (New York: Harcourt Brace Jovanovich, 1974), 142.

18 Tari Haahtela, in a lecture during "Science Days" at Helsinki University, January 15, 2011.

19 Wilson, *Biophilia*, 20.

20 Maurice Merleau-Ponty, *The Primacy of Perception* (Evanston, IL: Northwestern University Press, 1964), 162.

21 Albert Soesman, *Our Twelve Senses: Wellsprings of the Soul* (Stroud, Gloucestershire, UK: Hawthorn Press, 1998).

22 Colin St. John Wilson, "Architecture—Public Good and Private Necessity," *RIBA Journal* (March 1979).

23 Howard Gardner, *Intelligence Reframed: Multiple Intelligences for the 21st Century* (New York: Basic Books, 1999).

24 Mind you, this is a figure followed by seventeen zeros. Matti Bergström, *Aivojen fysiologiasta ja psyykestä* [On the physiology of the brain and psyche] (Helsinki: Porvoo, 1979), 77–78.

25 According to Edward O. Wilson, English words average two bits per letter. A single bacterium possesses about ten million bits of genetic information, a fungus a billion, and an insect from one to ten billion bits depending on the species. If the information in a single insect were translated into a code of English words and printed in standard size letters, the string would stretch over a thousand miles. Wilson, *Biophilia*, 16.

26 Semir Zeki, *Inner Vision: An Exploration of Art and the Brain* (Oxford: Oxford University Press, 1999), 1.

27 Ibid., 22.

28 Ibid., 2.

29 Gaston Bachelard, *The Poetics of Space* (Boston: Beacon Press, 1964), 6.

30 Karsten Harries, "Building and the Terror of Time," *Perspecta: The Yale Architectural Journal* 19 (1982).

31 Ezra Pound, *ABC of Reading* (New York: New Directions Publishing Company, 1987), 14.

32 Joseph Brodsky, *On Grief and Reason* (New York: Farrar, Straus & Giroux, 1995), 208.

33 Brodsky, "An Immodest Proposal," in *On Grief and Reason*, 207.

From the Beginning: Thirteen Questions

Glenn Murcutt, in discussion with Juhani Pallasmaa

Glenn Murcutt and Juhani Pallasmaa share a brotherly hug after their talk.

In St. John's Anglican Church in Lunenburg, Nova Scotia, the third and final keynote address, by Glenn Murcutt, was presented in a question and answer format, in contrast with the earlier keynote lectures by Kenneth Frampton and Juhani Pallasmaa.

Conference participants were asked to suggest the questions, which were then selected by Robert McCarter and Brian MacKay-Lyons. Juhani Pallasmaa, Glenn's "brother," was invited to take part as interviewer.

The church was packed to the gunwales by conference participants and the public, who were treated to a lively conversation against a backdrop of projected images of Glenn's work—a fitting conclusion to a historic event. Conference participants then wound down at the barn dance and bonfire before departing for home the morning after.

Juhani Pallasmaa: What made you decide to become an architect?

Glenn Murcutt: I grew up in a highly disciplined family in Papua New Guinea, where the value system was important. We got up at five o'clock in the summer—six o'clock in the winter—for a half mile run down to the swimming bath, a half mile swim before school, a half mile run back home. Then a shower, a jot of food, half an hour of music practice, and a two-kilometer walk to school. After school, Father would bring us down to swim another mile—followed by a hundred meters, and we had to break one minute. We'd go flat out and just get in under the minute, and he would say, "Do it again." We'd say, "We did what you asked." He'd say, "Do it again, and this time you've got to be faster." We knew if we didn't, we'd have to do it over and over. But he'd explain to us that in life you're going to think you've done everything you have to do, and you're going to be totally exhausted. But you've got to have staying power, the resilience to take you that much further.

Father was a joiner, a builder. He subscribed to all of these architectural magazines. In 1949 when I was thirteen years old, the Philip Johnson Glass House was published, and in 1952, Mies van der Rohe's Farnsworth House was published. My task was to read the article, after which I was questioned on every aspect. And if I didn't understand the question, he'd say, "Read the article again until you do understand." I'm telling you, I had no alternative—that's why I became an architect. In me, my father saw somebody who loved to draw, loved to build things. During school holidays, from the age of twelve, my brother and I worked in the joiner's shop where we built windows: box-frame windows, casement windows. We built staircases and cupboards, and even racing skiffs. By the time I was eighteen, I had built a skiff, rigged it, and made all the stainless steel fittings.

I was also raised to observe nature. My father always took me to places, showing me differences in natural form. He showed me how the Angophora costata, a most beautiful tree in Australia, grew into rock crevices; at a certain point, if there's a drought that branch will die, the last portion of it, but not before the tree shoots out another branch. That tree had such a humanlike skin on it, a humanlike form, and it had the most beautiful pink colors. Landscape became a very integral part of my thinking, and nature was so important to all of us. We were very conscious of not killing snakes. We were very conscious of the funnel-webbed spider—a very dangerous spider. I think a level of danger is necessary to keep your head sharp.

All of this is why I came to study architecture.

P You are not known for rushing through your work. How do you decide that a design is finished?

M It's finished when the client moves in! I've always been able to be self-critical without a lack of confidence—to stand back from the work and critique it. One of the greatest skills an architect can have is to know when the design is not good enough, and also to know when it's good enough to risk starting to build it. For the last twenty years I haven't made a single model, because I've trained myself to be able to visualize the work; I can understand the spaces, the light quality, the ventilation quality, the insect screen, and I understand the possibility of adjustments to all the systems. But there is no technique like being able to draw, to move that pencil across the paper and feel the insect screen going past on the rail, feel the thicker slatted screen, and then feel the glass move past. When you draw, you're thinking three-dimensionally the whole time.

In the early years I made models. My uncle had given me, at the age of twelve, a book on the principles of flight, and I made many model gliders and sailboats—which prepared me later in life to make a judgment about a building so that I know if I've sited it correctly. I know where the wind would normally come over the top of the hill; if instead it comes around the house, it's going to come around here and move back. So, I'd analyze the site. I'd use a clinometer to measure the trees. I'd have the ground tested to understand the soil content and the rock level, which can tell me a lot about the potential height of a tree. If I know what age the tree is approximately and to what dimensions it will grow, I can see how the house could be placed in relation to that tree. You look at the water table, the hydrology patterns. You look at the soil patterns. You look at the flora and the fauna. You're looking at how flora impact the landscape, at how insects impact the flora. You look at the fauna in relation to the insects. You make sure you aren't disturbing any insect life patterns. These are all things to be considered—I use a list of seventy things, in fact.

Remember, Australia ranges from 12 degrees south of the equator down to 47 degrees south of the equator. And we're the width of the United States, the height of the United States, and possibly the area of the United States. So we've got monsoonal tropics, subtropics, warm temperate, temperate, cool temperate; we've got coastal, we've got mountains; we've got the snow, the arid, the hot arid—we've got so many climatic zones. If I've taken into account nearly all of the seventy things on my list, I know I'm pretty close to a finished design.

When we did the Arthur Boyd Centre in Riversdale, Australia, we did not do a single elevation of the project until the last week. Everything was worked on in section. When you do a section vertically and a section horizontally, you visualize what the space will be like. You visualize how you frame the view, how the louver blades also pick up the northeast and southeast winds from the coast. You know they pick up light in the winter morning, bouncing off one of the blades to the inside. The building was not designed from the point of view of elevation. It was designed in relation to the site: the site contours, the flood level, the runoff coming in from the back, water storage. All these sorts of things were taken into account.

P The problem of architecture is the problem of the house. Do you agree?

M Aldo van Eyck said, "The leaf is to the tree as the house is to the city." The house is so much more complicated than a multistory office building. The built form of any city or any community is the manifestation of the values, the culture of the day. So it is the whole society that is responsible for the quality of the architecture. Now, the house is a really complicated issue, and it's central to architecture. If you look at the work of Mies, of Le Corbusier, of any architect, you will find that some of their very best work came from the house. The house is where one understands the social relationships of the family—the parents to one another and to the children, the children to the parents, the neighbor to the neighbor, and the house to the street. These relationships are all embodied in the house. When I think of Alvar Aalto's Säynätsalo Town Hall—which is one of his great buildings and complexes, and one of the greatest anywhere, anytime—it seems essentially domestic in nature; it comes from Aalto's understanding of the house and is in many ways the house of the community.

I have a great love of the house, because I have a great love of the people for whom I design houses. It was such a joy to do a house for the Marika-Alderton family, who were Aboriginal clients. Culturally, the Aboriginal people have to be able to look out of a house and not be seen inside. The parents live at the western end of the house, and the children live to the east. This design was absolutely critical. At the end of the day, the sun is sinking, dying, and the parents are closer to death; the children are to the east because it's the beginning of the day, it's the future. The house can hold up to fourteen people from time to time, when the extended family comes from another part of the region, but they don't just come knocking on the door. They sit outside the house, waiting to be welcomed. The screens are slats of 25 mm, with a 10 mm gap. In the sunlight, an absolutely amazing thing happens: the slats, instead of reading as 25 mm thick, read as 10 mm, and the 10 mm gap reads as 25 mm. The light is so intense that the darkness shrinks and the light expands. You can look up and see the horizon, which is very important, you can see the weather pattern changing, the animals going past, the whales, the seagulls—whatever is the natural pattern in this location in the Northern Territory. I think the Aboriginal people have survived not through being the fittest but through cooperation, and the house represents that.

The Marika-Alderton House is a way to think about a house in that part of the world. Now, in Sydney a house is a very different thing. The house is much more about, for example, arriving, entering, greeting, moving, receiving, then eating, discussing, preparing, cleaning, parting; the experience is much more transitory compared with the Aboriginal people. Every group has a cultural background that shapes how they think about a house.

P Can you speak about moments in your work when craft springs from culture?

M Today, about one in twenty-eight Australians has some Italian blood. Melbourne has the second largest Greek population in the world. So when we speak of Australian culture, we are very mixed. In Australia we also have some marvelous builders; I've worked for twenty-five years with builders who came from Finland, from a culture that values craft. And we have some beautiful timbers—five of the eight most durable timbers in the world, most of them native to the east and north coasts of Australia. In the south we have fine timber such as celery top pine and Huon pine—you look at that grain and you could eat it.

Craft is very important. I learned from Aalto that if you have a metal door handle that is in the sun, or in subzero temperatures, then you can burn your hand or your hand would stick to it in the cold; to wrap that door handle in leather, as Aalto does, is a beautiful thing. The crafting makes such a huge difference. A column in a room of Aalto's, wrapped in cane, is a beautiful thing, because to lean up against cane is more beautiful than to lean up against metal. Where the materials are and how you use them: that makes beautiful crafting.

But crafting can only assist in the design; it can't be a thing in itself. Design must come first: understanding the nature of the place, the nature of the materials, the climatic conditions. All those things make the hydrology, the morphology, the geology, water table, flora, fauna, history, aboriginal history, European history. Once you start understanding all those things, you start to get an idea about the place making.

My real interest is in very well built buildings. I get it well built by going to the site when the builders are there. You see some beautiful work being done, as well as some terrible stuff. The last thing you want to do is go to the terrible stuff and say to the tradesperson, "This is absolutely shocking, we have just got to fix it"—because then you demoralize that person. You are going to work from the beautiful stuff. You ask the builder, "Who's the one who has done this? This is absolutely fantastic. If you keep that standard up on the job, it will just be wonderful," and you say nothing more. It's very important to understand the tradespeople who do the work, so they aren't demoralized, so that they will give the best of themselves. There is nothing more meaningful for a tradesperson who does something well than to be recognized for it. On my jobs, I've had builders who drove three hours south from Sydney to do a building. They didn't have to do it but they wanted to, and the builders would get their families to come down on weekends to have a look at what they were doing. That is how buildings get beautifully crafted.

P You describe the kind of relationship of mutual respect and friendship between an architect and a builder that is becoming rare today.
M One of the things I say to a new builder is that there is no such thing as a silly question.

P If you could make one change in the education of an architect, what would it be?
M Growing up, nature and conservation were very important to us. At the age of twelve, the boys in the family were each given a piece of timber and were shown how to square it up, using wire and sticks to turn this rough piece of timber into something beautiful. Our pocket money wasn't a given; we earned it only when we did something we weren't asked to do, or if we'd asked a very good question. We learned the importance of waste. If you left the light on in the house in a room you were not using, you were fined threepence each time. When we got a case of oranges from the markets, we'd have to sort through them: those will be eaten tomorrow, those the next day, those the day after that. Everything was about avoiding waste and ensuring that you'd have something left for tomorrow. So, when I began my architectural education, I knew the real principles behind conservation, to be able to use only that which is necessary and leave enough for tomorrow. If I taught building and construction full-time, I would assign the whole first year to a program related to nature in this sense.

When I was in school, a full one and a half terms were devoted to understanding continuity in nature. We had to discuss questions, such as: how does a branch of a tree join the tree, and how does it stay there? I don't think that many people know how a branch joins a tree, but if you're ever in an old pine forest that has already been cut and there are a few branches left, have a look. Those branches look as if somebody's speared them into the trunk—right in the heart of it is the heartwood of the branch. It is the most beautiful thing. When a ficus tree grows tall and the branches get too heavy, it sends aerial roots down. In northern Australia they take bamboo, drill out the center, and put soil in it; they put this as a prop under a low tree branch and water it, and the aerial root grows through the bamboo in three months and gets into the ground. Within a year and a half that root is stabilizing the tree. In many ways it is how the Japanese might think about stabilizing a tree. What a beautiful construction!

How does the spider spin its web? How does it hold its weight? The spider sends down the first beautiful trail, then tightens it, and then drops down and does a couple of moves up and back until it gets the center point—and then it starts spinning on this center point, around and around and around. It is fantastic. The strength of a spider's web is its elasticity.

You can learn about how foundations work, for example, by how tree root systems work. To understand composite construction is very important. The nature of timber is that it is very good with compression, not so good with tension. Steel, on the other hand, is very good with tension, not so good with compression. Make a flitch plate beam with steel inside timber, and you'll get a beautiful beam out of it. It works like muscles and sinews on the body, the summation of two materials working beautifully together.

So the first thing I would do with young architects is keep them away from building altogether, and instead introduce architecture and construction through nature.

P What is your greatest hope for the future of architecture?

M My greatest hope for the future would be that architecture finds a sense of responsibility—an ethic in design, in the use of materials, and toward the population and the poorer peoples of the world—such as I have found in working with the Aboriginal people in Australia. Another hope of mine is that the computer will be used in the way it should be. Most computer-generated buildings, in my view, are megastructures that are supposed to do everything for everybody, and they are the most unethical things I have ever seen. I dislike them intensely. I love modern architecture, I love the structure of architecture, and I think the computer can be used in a way that assists the engineer. Here I think the computer is absolutely the most fantastic instrument. The setsquare and the T-square were marvelous instruments. But they were used as instruments, not as methods of design.

P What advice or guidance would you offer for young architects?

M Work with very good people. As my father used to say, it is not a case of what money you get when you work for an architect, it is a case of getting the best experience.

Find the architect you most admire, look at their work, see where they're doing buildings, and see if you can get a job on a site. I believe in getting your hands dirty as an architect. To know the processes of construction, to know the building—this is our language. If you don't understand how the materials are going to work, if you don't understand the nature of the materials, then you don't have an architect's vocabulary. The language of architecture also has to include the nature of materials. Louis Kahn asked about a brick: What does it want to be? A brick doesn't want to go into tension, it wants to go into compression—one brick laid upon another, on another, on another. You can put brick into an arch, or you can use it in combination with other materials, such as steel. But the nature of brick is that it is a compressive material, and if you understand that, it starts to become part of the vocabulary of your architecture. This vocabulary is extremely important.

My father once said to me, "Son, remember now that you are beginning your practice, you must start off the way you would like to finish. Further, for every compromise you make in your work, the result represents the quality of your next client." This statement is not about arrogance. Compromise means doing something that you know you ought not to be doing. Most good clients will have a very good reason for not liking something, which gives you the opportunity of making it better.

I was raised on Henry David Thoreau, who said the mass of humanity lead lives of quiet desperation. Since most of us are going to be doing things in our lives, the most important thing is to do those things extraordinarily well. Don't be in a rush to be an architect. Let it come. If you can travel, go and see the work—there is no better education. And traveling in another country allows you to see your own country more clearly. You see it afresh. You can get quite blinded by your own environment. Go away! When you come back, you shall understand your own place better.

P When does a building become architecture?

M When it becomes art. It is all about appropriateness. It is ethics, life quality, integrity, prospect, refuge. It is the ability to open up, close down, and work with the seasons. You have to capture the environment, as well as project it. In the house, if you see how the windows operate, the air can pass through the rooms. I can open up vents, so that the rain comes down and I get the smell of rain coming in—that beautiful, fresh smell of rain. To hear the sound of rain falling on the roof is just beautiful. To be able to sit at your desk and have the air caress you while you write, yet not disturb your papers. To be able to look beyond and see a prospect—the building starts at the frame, at the outlook, and shows you where you are in this environment, so that you understand the section of the building from the place where you're sitting. That is really very beautiful.

The house is an instrument that is being played by nature, so that the people who live there can understand the time of the day, the weather, the season. It's all part of the building as a frame for the way you live. The animals are part of your life. To see the most beautiful birds come through, the galahs and the sulphur-crested cockatoos, is very important. To allow nature to feed through this instrument with you as the audience. A house like this has a level of simplicity and a level of, if I may say, elegance, and it is very achievable, economically.

If you make sure that your first job is really well done, you will be surprised how quickly the next job comes along.

P What building in history would you have been most proud to have designed?
M In history? The pyramids seem quite good.

P Can you explain the origins and evolution of your architectural language?
M Having studied in my very early youth the work of Philip Johnson's Glass House and Mies van der Rohe's Farnsworth House, I spent probably six years trying to get them out of my system. However, when visiting the Farnsworth House about four years ago, I went into the shower room and found that the whole of the mechanical services were on the other side of the shower—you had to walk through the shower to get to them—and I thought, my God, I would fail a student for such an offense! I learned from that. We're plugged in to think these buildings are the ultimate, but they all have their faults; the things that haven't worked in those buildings seem very significant to me.

On the other hand, I have to tell you about going to Pierre Chareau's Maison de Verre in Paris in 1973. I was very interested in modernism. There was a logic about it. But the brilliance of the Maison de Verre, which was built for a doctor, for me was the release from modernism. It was a contraption. It had all these moving parts. When the doctor was saying goodbye to the women patients, who were often quite pregnant, he'd pull a handle from inside his office and make the door slide open without having to go out there and stand to the side as the patient walked past. It was a remarkable building, as modern when I saw it as it was in 1928. I still think it's an incredibly modern building, a great piece of architecture that has the most amazing integrity in detail through the space. And yet my work isn't the Maison de Verre. What that building did is help me understand for what reasons it was done. It's of its day, and also before and beyond, and it's going to continue to be relevant.

In California I spent time with Craig Ellwood, who said to me, "I am just one of the three blind Mies." The United States led the world in technology, and there was this really fantastic glass and the gaskets were so great that no water came in. I asked Craig, how do you keep the climate control in this house? He looked at me and said, "By the air conditioning." I felt so stupid. It turned me away entirely from air conditioning, which is the lazy way of living in a house.

Understanding how to have the wind come into the house the way you want is so important, so that when the wind is blowing in a certain direction and you want to direct it, you can open up the roof here and there, and create positive fresh air over here, negative fresh air there. I realized that there was no future for me in looking at such work, so I started taking on all those things I'd learned about nature: about place-making, materiality, colors, collection of water, waste management. I try to work within the cultural language of a built-up environment, so I work in typology, I work in materiality, I work with section, and I work with heart. I work with all these things.

P Do you think the desire to be closer to nature is expressed through the construction of highly detailed primitive huts?

M When Luis Barragán received the Pritzker Prize, there was quite an outcry about his rather small works. I remember that Arthur Drexler said in Barragán's defense, "When you see the work, it hits you with a wallop." You learn so much from what Barragán has done—his beauty, his simplicity. Barragán himself often said, "Any work of architecture that is designed without serenity in mind is in my view a mistake." Works that have a level of freedom in them can influence a whole group of buildings.

All young architects: when you build your first house, no matter where it is, keep your eye on it if you like it, because you might get a chance to buy it. That way you can avoid having to design a house for yourself. The major problem with architects designing their own houses is that they're trying to achieve everything. When you design for someone else, you know you can't achieve everything; you have to identify a few very good ideas and reinforce those ideas right down to the last detail. To select a door handle or a lock, those sorts of things, the small things—they're the details that carry the design through beautifully.

P Can you talk about your approach to designs set within the city?

M My approach is concerned with the same principles as any design. Where does the wind come from? Where does the rain come from, and when does it come? What is the water table, the typology, the morphology? What is the materiality, the scale, the proportions, and how do I work within this context, so that the building has a very, very established place in which to be? If done right, the air coming in is fresh and beautiful. The building has a roof that comes up and captures the breezes, and the house lets the air through, and the morning sunlight comes through. Design in the city has the same principles as any design, so what you have to do is ask: What are the principles? When you understand the principles and the place, and you ask the appropriate questions, then you'll probably find a very good answer.

PROJECTS

Texts by Robert McCarter

Deborah Berke Partners

Deborah Berke
New York, New York

Deborah Berke's work is largely placed in the urban context, often involving adaptive reuse of existing buildings. Her works exhibit an acute sensitivity to the nuances and qualities of existing contexts, and the importance of light, sound, material, and scale in calibrating and choreographing daily urban life. Avoiding the too common tendency to formally express the presence of the new addition in the old context, her subtle insertions and transformations present modest exterior facades to the street. Emphasizing the importance of "the everyday" over the exceptional, Berke's work can be said to exhibit a true democratic spirit. She is especially attentive to the concept of personal space—what each dweller calls "my place"—and the photographs of her buildings show them inhabited, rather than reduced to purely formal compositions. Not involved primarily in landscape place-making, Berke works in urban places, the cosmopolitan place of the city, where each site is at once both unique and generalized. Within the city her works achieve a quality of domesticity and interiority that are increasingly rare in today's world.

Learning from Autopia
Irwin Union Bank
Columbus, IN, 2006

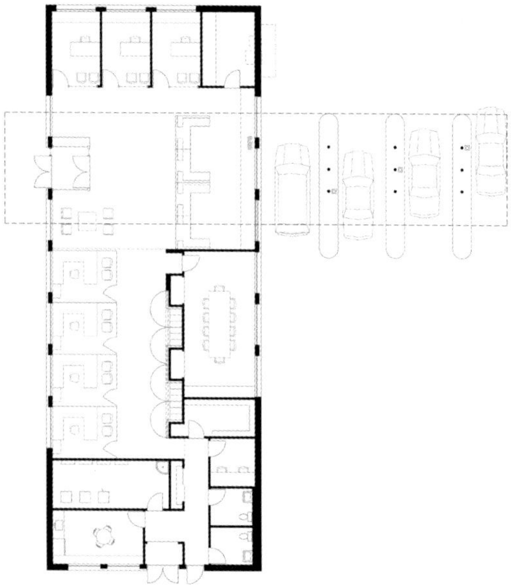

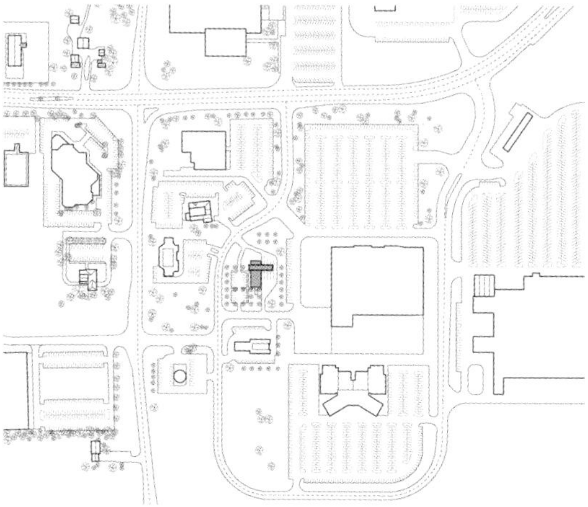

Irwin Union Bank

Marlon Blackwell Architect

Marlon Blackwell
Fayetteville, Arkansas

Marlon Blackwell seeks to engage the concrete experiences of everyday life in the designs for his buildings. He sees "the vernacular as a familiar face, reflecting our values and our relationship with a place, its culture, and its environment." Seeking to intensify this condition, his buildings often involve the playful confluence and unexpected intertwining of the natural and the man-made. In inhabiting his buildings, one can "rediscover" the natural context, experiencing it as if for the first time, realizing Cézanne's statement, "One must see nature as no one has seen it before." Blackwell engages the material cultural of his local context in northwest Arkansas, making moving works from the most modest means, including "trash." His projects often involve extending the life of existing buildings through transformations of program in sensitive yet spatially assertive additions and renovations. This follows from his belief that we need "to reuse what we already have." Grounded in the particularities of his context, Blackwell's buildings are invariably transformative of our experience of that place—a fusion of space, material, light, and landscape into a construction of beauty.

Biomimicry

Ruth Lilly Visitor's Pavilion,
Indianapolis, IN, 2010

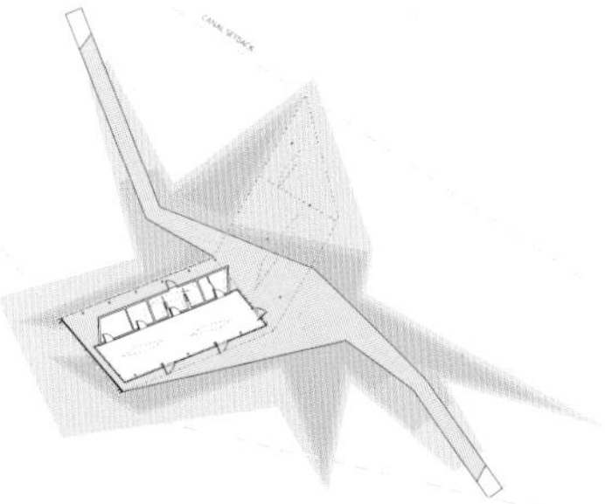

Wendell Burnette Architects

Wendell Burnette
Phoenix, Arizona

Wendell Burnette is an architect whose intensity of crafting space is exceptional, yet whose starting point is his belief that the specificity of a place or context is the most important material for design. This sensitivity to the subtleties of the natural context is complemented by his minimal designs, which both respond to and engage their places. Burnette's formally minimal interventions (paradoxically) result in experientially maximal possibilities for the inhabitants. Exceptionally attentive to the character of the materials with which he builds, Burnette has produced a contemporary American construction craft, thoughtfully fabricated and carefully detailed, from the most modest and readily available materials. In this way, his work may be said to be both practical, involving minimal energy use and sustainable practices, and poetic, allowing enrichment of experience through engagement of the senses. For Burnette, the architect's primary task is "learning to see the place" in which one works. Yet the lessons learned in one's place are by no means limited to that place, and his locally appropriate architecture has meaning for the larger world.

Big Box Minimalism

Palo Verde Library/
Maryvale Community Center,
Phoenix, AZ, 2005

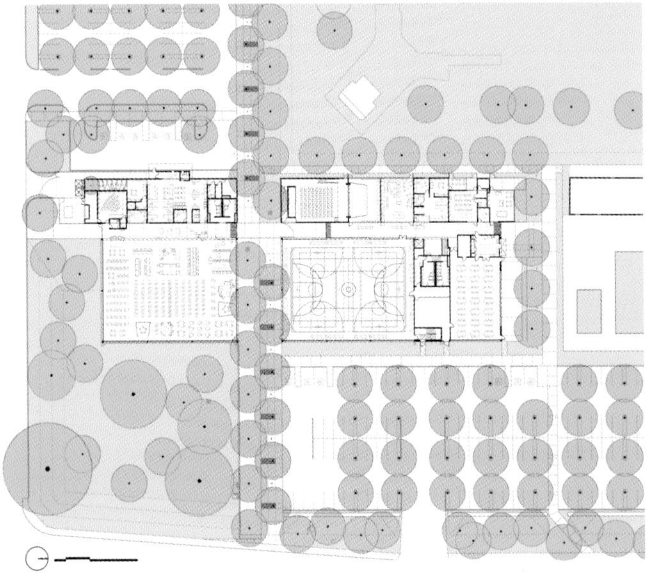

32'
24'
16'
12'
8'

Ghost Architectural Laboratory

Upper Kingsburg, Nova Scotia

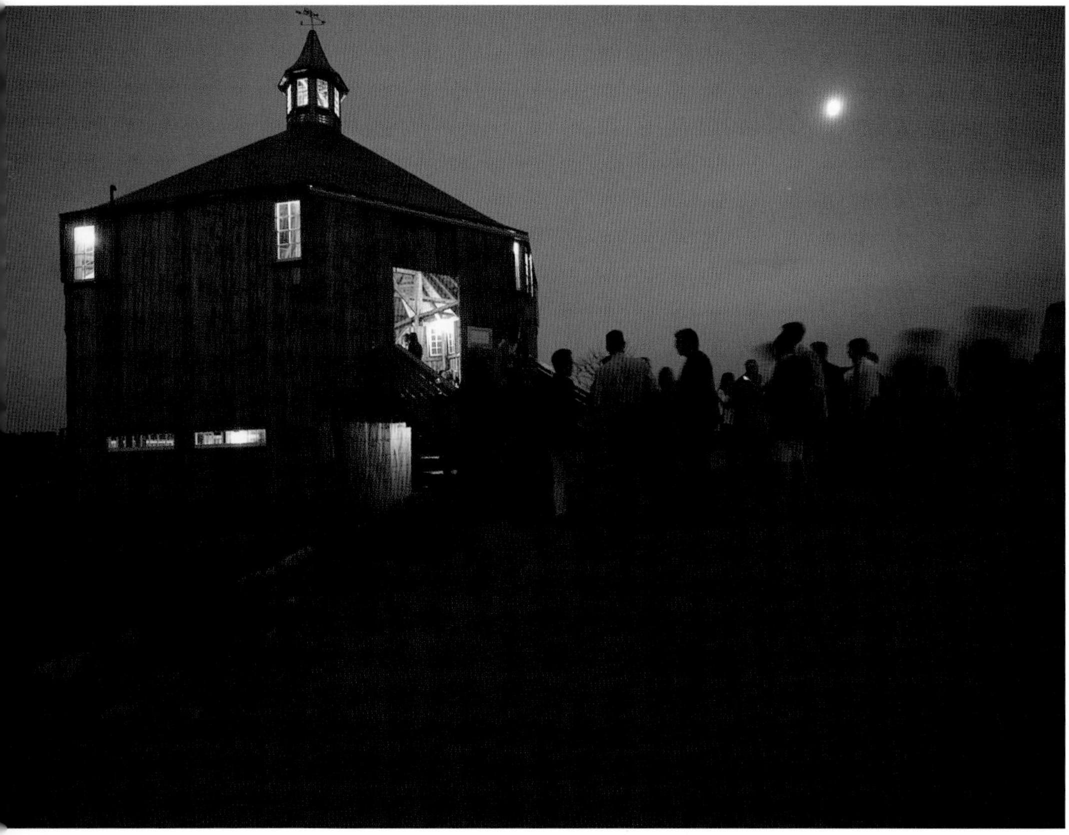

Sited at the LaHave River estuary on Nova Scotia's Atlantic coast, where Samuel de Champlain made his first landfall in the new world in 1604, the Ghost Architectural Laboratory was started in 1994 by Brian MacKay-Lyons. In its thirteen iterations, it served as an international education center in the building arts, as well as a constructive critique of contemporary architectural education. The resulting campus, built in and around the foundations of previous structures, is an expression of utopian architectural ambitions, constructed with the most modest means. The structures are constructed using traditional local building techniques and renewable materials from nearby sawmills, and like the vernacular farmhouses, barns, and boathouses of Nova Scotia, are sustainable in every possible meaning of the word. As a place of learning through making with your own hands, and through collaborating with others, the Ghost Lab enacts Giambattista Vico's aphorism, *verum ipsum factum*; "we only know what we have made." As MacKay-Lyons notes, "By 'listening' to the site's rich history and local material culture traditions, yet 'willing' buildings that are clearly modern, the Ghost Lab is a built critical regionalist argument."

Old Ghosts

Previous: Troop Barn, by Ghost Lab 11, Upper Kingsburg, 2009

This page: Sheep Shed, by Ghost Lab 9, Upper Kingsburg, 2007

Ghost Lantern, by Ghost Lab 1, Upper Kingsburg, 1999

Ghost Towers, by Ghost Lab 6, Upper Kingsburg, 2004

Ghost 8 Studio, by Ghost Lab 8, Upper Kingsburg, 2006

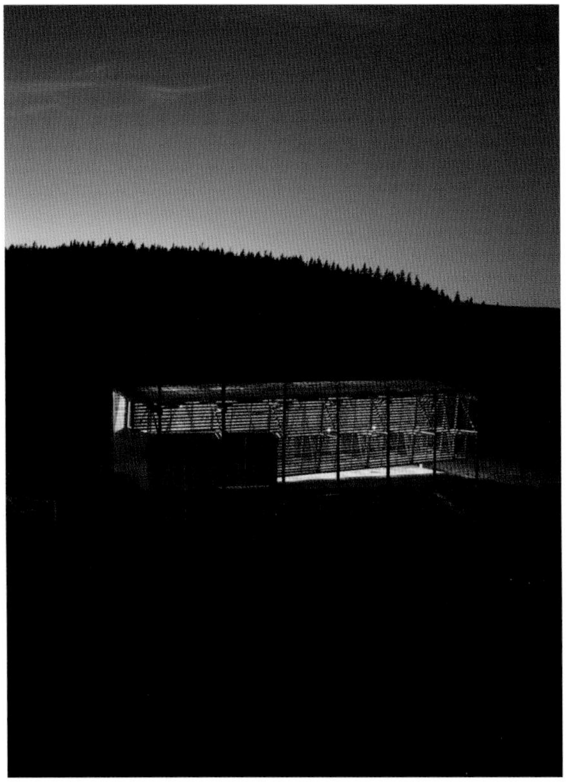

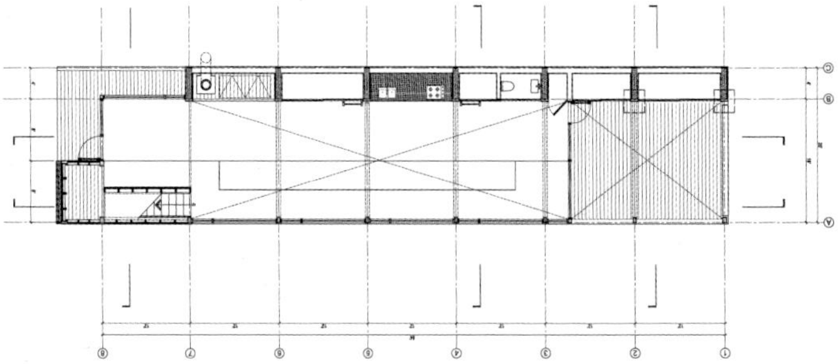

Pavilion, by Ghost Lab 5,
Upper Kingsburg, 2003

Cabins, by Ghost Lab 7,
Upper Kingsburg, 2005

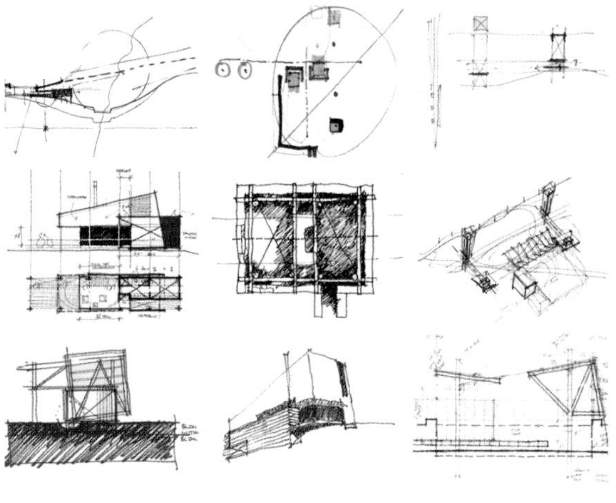

Local Architecture

Jersey Devil Design/Build

Steve Badanes
United States

Principal of Jersey Devil, Steve Badanes established one of the very first contemporary design-build practices, which he has continued now for forty peripatetic years. He is also involved in organizing several academic design-build programs around the United States, most recently for the University of Washington in Seattle and in Mexico. In both his practice and teaching, he has endeavored to continue the sense of urgency generated by the energy crisis of the early 1970s, and the impact this had on principles of architectural practice. He has also learned from and engaged local vernacular building practices where they offered alternatives to energy-expending technology, such as his use of the traditional "Cracker House" morphology to minimize or eliminate the need for air-conditioning in his Florida works. Badanes's works indicate how, as he says, "small projects of high quality, far from the centers of media and culture, can have a positive impact on the larger society." His work has exemplified the belief that "the profession needs to be more proactive"—in general, and, in particular, in addressing contemporary architecture's failure to be sustainable in every meaning of the word.

Psychedelic
Previous: Natchez Street Beach Pavilion, Seaside, FL, 1993

This spread, left to right: Fremont Troll, Seattle, 1990

Inflatables, Princeton, NJ, Bubble Day, 1969

Bleachers, Danny Woo Community Garden, 2007

Next spread: Community quilt, Danny Woo Community Garden, Seattle, 1989–present

Rick Joy
Tucson, Arizona

Rick Joy Architect

Rick Joy is an architect and, early on, was a builder. His designs present a clear response to the climate, landscape, and local material culture. He makes buildings that live well in their place, and are lived in well by their inhabitants. This is a slow process, requiring both patience and perseverance on the part of the architect, and has nothing to do with the search for recognition and fame. Grounded initially in the desert, where what he calls a "divine light" already exists and can be incorporated as part of the building's "materials," Joy has more recently taken the lessons of the desert to different contexts. For Joy, the design of a home is the architect's most important task, and he believes that "experience of place, presence of mind, authenticity of spirit, and genuineness of origins are at the root of making the architecture of enthusiastic dwelling at home in a specific place." Joy's architecture is intended to be "a revelation of the real," where the atmospheric qualities of a place and the rich material and sensorial experience of daily inhabitation are synthesized in the making of the building.

Minimum
Woodstock Farm,
Woodstock, VT, 2009

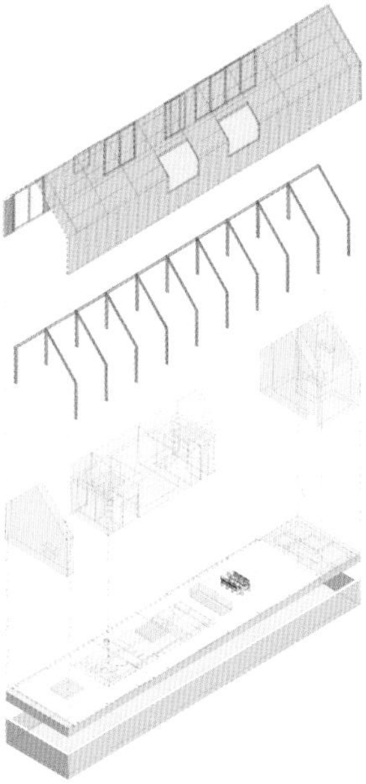

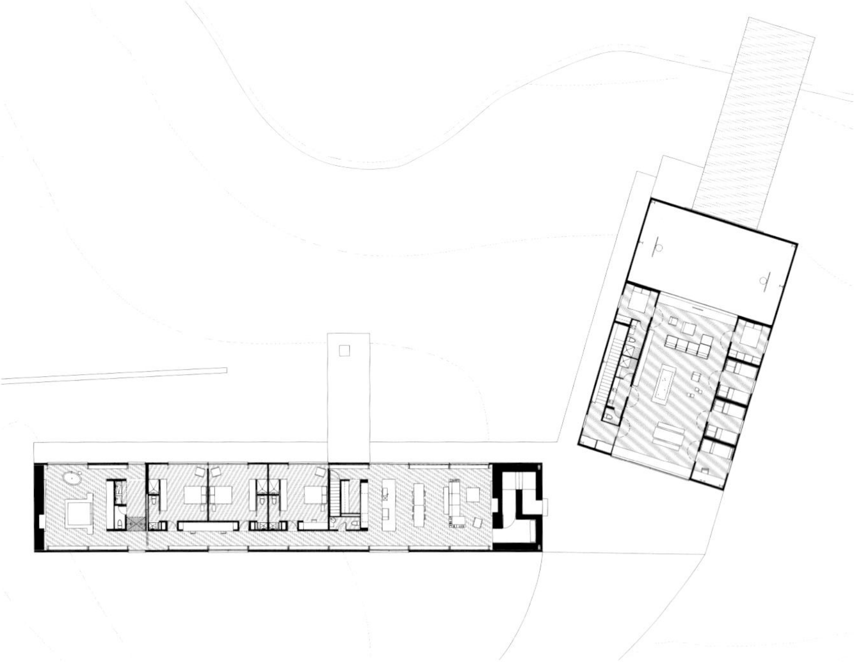

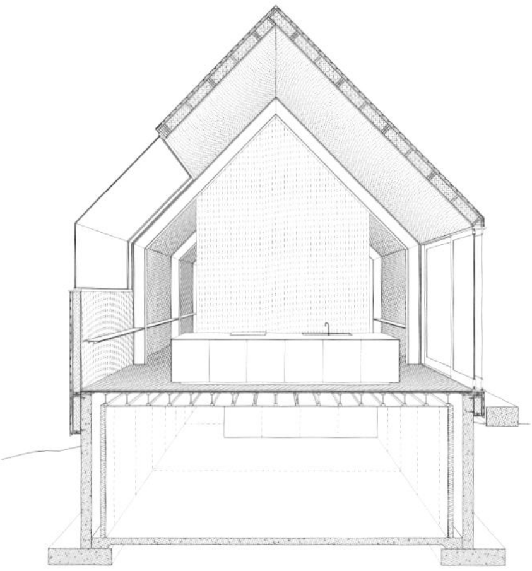

Kéré Architecture

Francis Kéré
Berlin and Burkina Faso

Francis Kéré's architecture is architecture of the earth in its purest form; like the mud buildings of the Dogon region (which neighbors his native Burkina Faso), his work approaches the "absolute zero" of architecture. Trained in Germany, he combines contemporary western scientific knowledge with traditional African building techniques to overcome local challenges, resulting in innovative cooling systems achieved with locally available materials; clay brick walls with overhanging corrugated metal roofs supported by reinforcing bar trusses allow airflow between roof and ceiling. By "respond[ing] to the extreme climate conditions and to use locally abundant materials, emphasis is set on the village's potential: material and labor are found within the community, ensuring the sustainability of the project." Of critical importance is the fact that Kéré's "philosophy goes beyond sustainable design and encompasses an essential development aspect: integrating the villagers in the process, the project spurs empowerment. The people gain vital skills as they are confronted with the responsibility of building a brighter future for the next generations." Kéré's architecture grows directly out of the minimal materials and maximal spirit of his own community.

Testing
Secondary School and Library, Gando, 2007

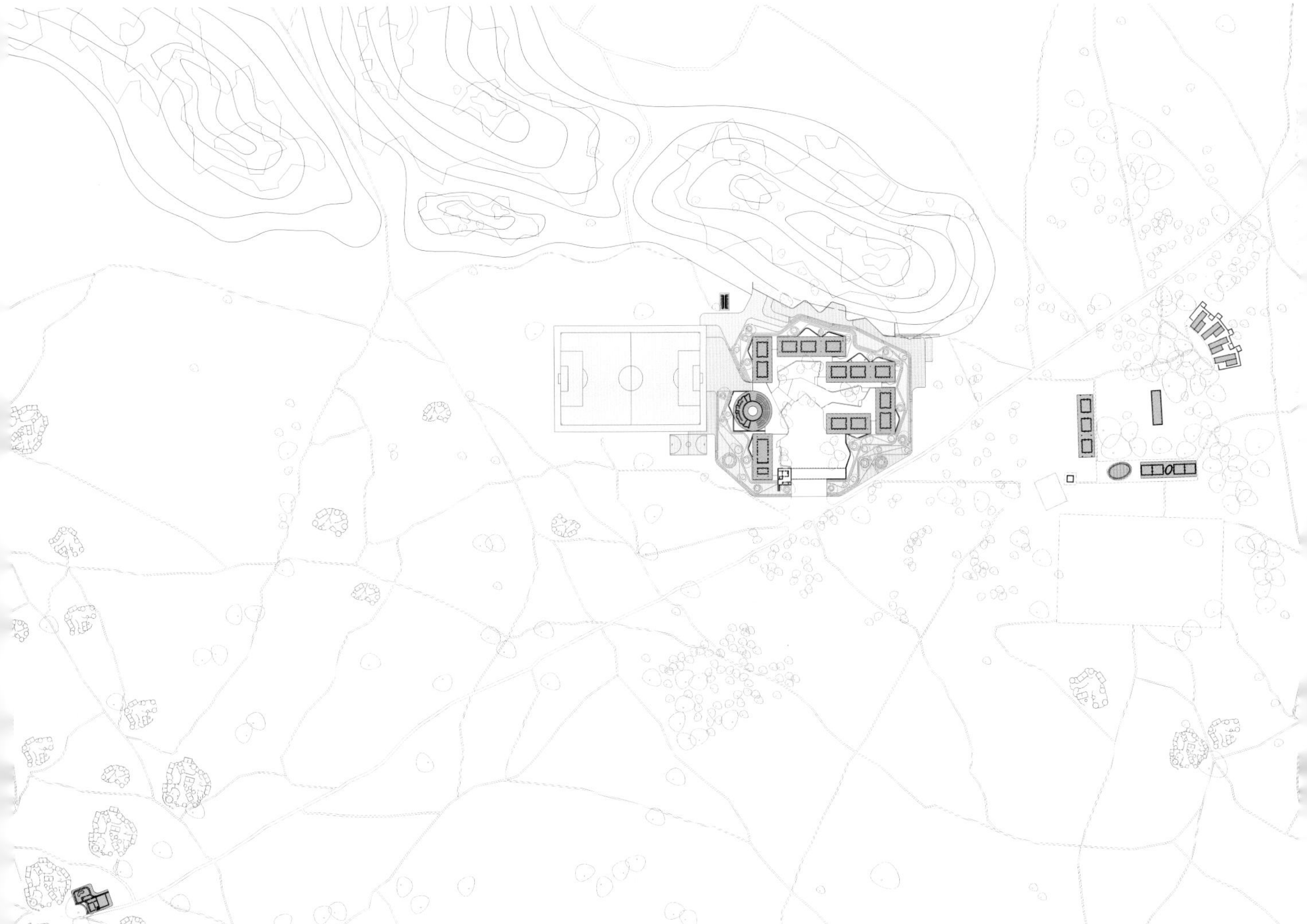

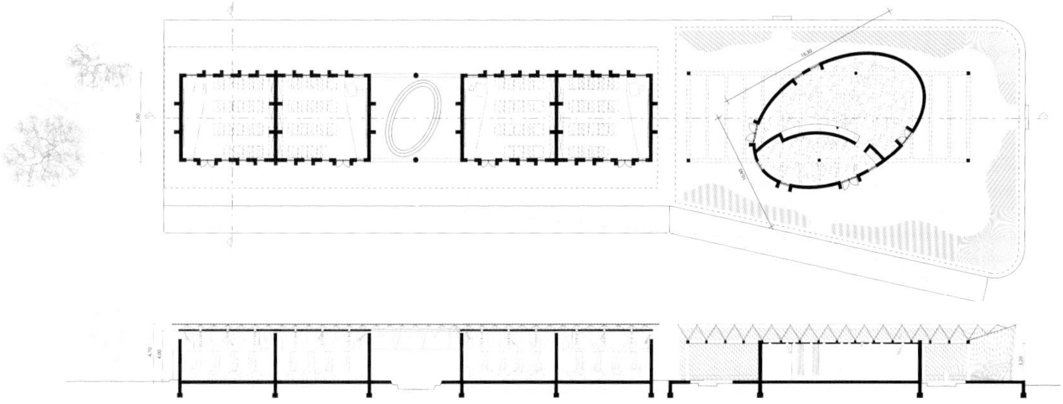

Richard Kroeker Design

Richard Kroeker
Halifax, Nova Scotia

Richard Kroeker's designs exemplify his longstanding engagement with and commitment to the First Nations of Canada, and may be understood as a part of the modern search for the anthropological origins of architecture. In determining both where and how to build new structures, he begins with a careful study of the remnants of previous inhabitants. Inspired by the structure of the birch bark canoe, first made at the time of the pyramids, "the essential strategy in this work is to do more with less. Making this instrumental connection gives solidity to cultural survival and renewal." Employing the human body as the measuring and dimensioning template, his constructions often take the form of assembled forest components, which are built not from construction drawings, but as a series of sequential steps, each a scaffolding for the next. Kroeker's buildings connect with a range of people from the most advanced structural engineers in the world to his recent work with the Mi'kmaq community, as a "result [of] on an ongoing study of how indigenous approaches can inform contemporary design."

Native Material Culture
Previous: Beaverbank, Beaverbank, Nova Scotia, 1998

This spread: Pictou Landing Health Center, Pictou Landing First Nation, Canada, 2008

Olson Kundig Architects

Tom Kundig
Seattle, Washington

In Tom Kundig's architecture, the expression of the craft of making, and its engagement in experience, engenders a quality of built character absent from much contemporary construction. He believes that "building craft is the confluence and resolution of natural, cultural, and economic forces." His architecture actively engages the fact that today the act of building remains largely accomplished by handwork, allowing the making of adjustments and changes during construction. His small domestic projects, often built in the fragile environment of the Pacific Northwest, are examples of exquisite architecture made using the most basic materials and construction methods. Kundig endeavors to support and continue local craft traditions as opposed to accepting their replacement by digital prefabrication, believing that hand craft involves risk while digital fabrication is inherently risk-free. His work accepts and engages the anomalies that occur on the building site, the naturally occurring and all too human imperfections in craft. He believes that the architect and craftsman's sense of proportion, fit, and finish are essential to the creation of experientially enriching places.

Carving
The Pierre, San Juan
Islands, WA, 2010

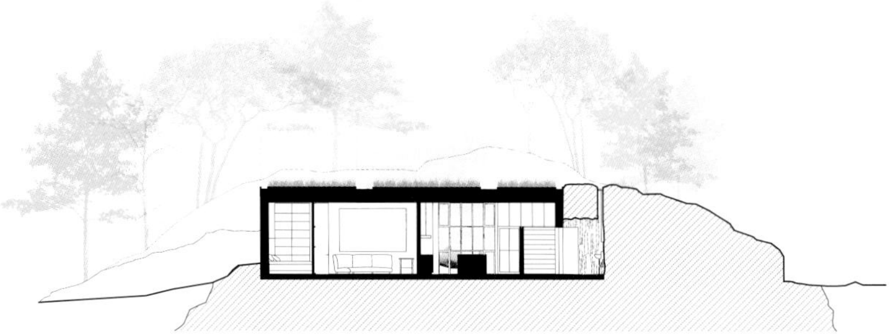

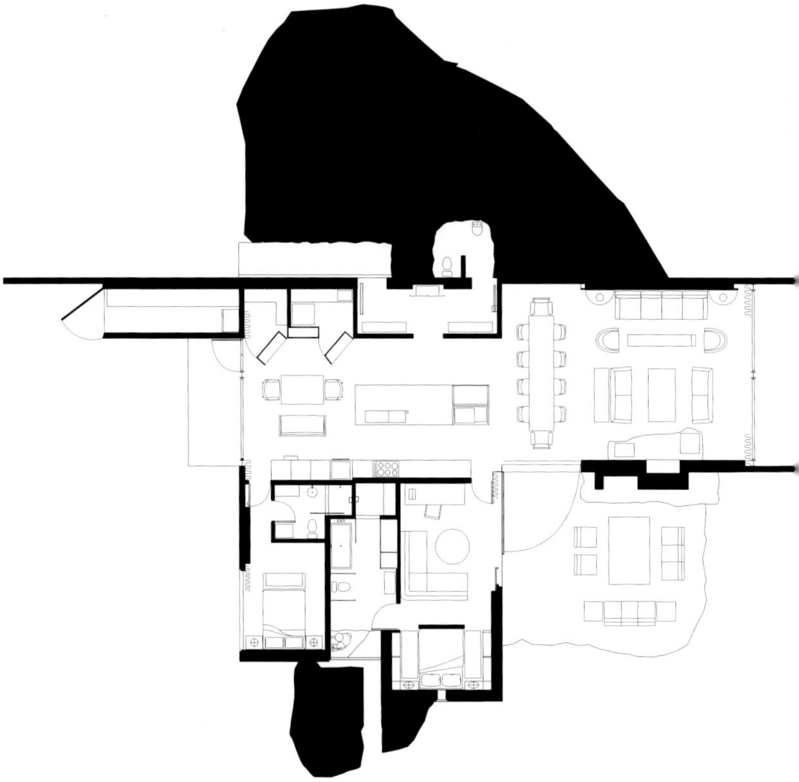

Lake | Flato Architects

Ted Flato
San Antonio, Texas

Ted Flato learns from his predecessors and from both architectural and industrial vernacular constructions, which respond directly to climate and material culture. Lake | Flato believes that designing for a particular place is inherently sustainable, and their projects span from the domestic to the public scale. They believe that the making of courtyard and landscape spaces is equally important to the making of enclosed spaces, and they construct naturally ventilated and shaded spaces that engage their inhabitants in the qualities of the local climate. Their projects reusing local waste products, such as recycled oil-field pipe, achieve the quality of being irreducible and essential. They state that, "architecture should be rooted in its particular place in the world...Using local materials and partnering with the best local craftsmen, we sought to create buildings that are tactile and modern, environmentally responsible and authentic, artful and crafted." Their work recognizes that the fundamental elements of architecture change only very slowly over time, and that how people have inhabited the local landscape in the past remains of greatest relevance today.

Sustainable Practices
Recycled Oil Field Pipes

Air Barns,
San Saba, TX, 1999

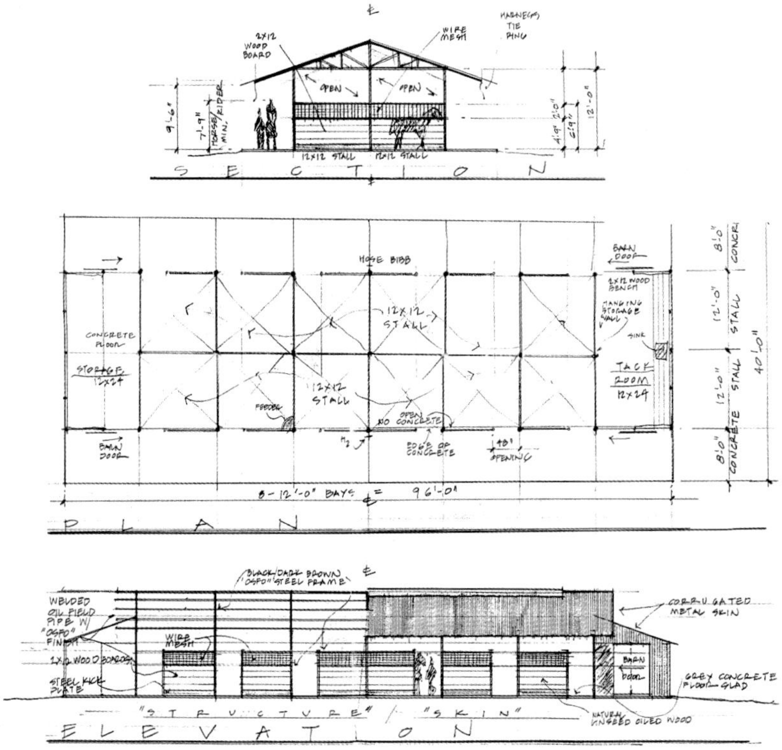

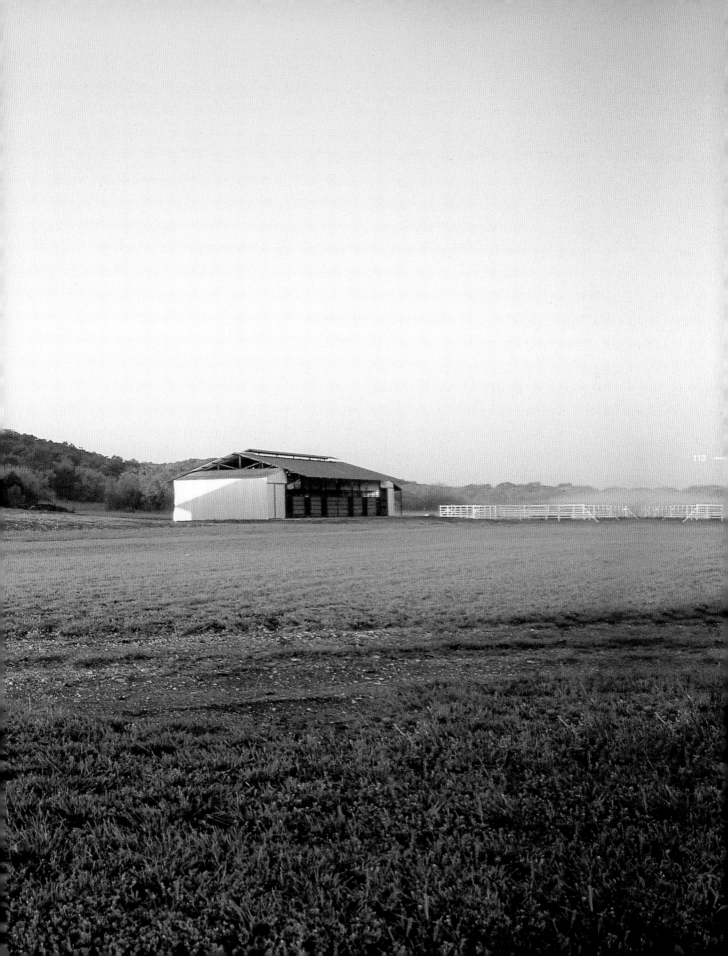

Brian MacKay-Lyons
Halifax, Nova Scotia

MacKay-Lyons Sweetapple Architects

MacKay-Lyons Sweetapple's architecture is the result of both "listening to the place" and "willing paradise" into existence. To a degree increasingly rare in today's world, their work is grounded in its local place, with its uniquely volatile climate, landscape, and material culture. They feel themselves to be part of both local tradition and universal modernism, in that they cite Frank Lloyd Wright's building six hundred houses using only four "types," as well as noting, "the vernacular is always up-to-date." Each of their projects involves the ordinary and the extraordinary, the local and the universal, the circumstantial and the archetypal. Learning from their place, MacKay-Lyons Sweetapple believes that "the landscape is the project," and that agriculture and architecture are parallel ways of cultivating the land. Their houses are "landscape-viewing devices," providing both prospect and refuge, and they endeavor to make their buildings become an integral part of their place. Having empathy for the world, and a desire to improve it, as well as anger at the state it is in, they believe that "you should leave the world a better place than you found it."

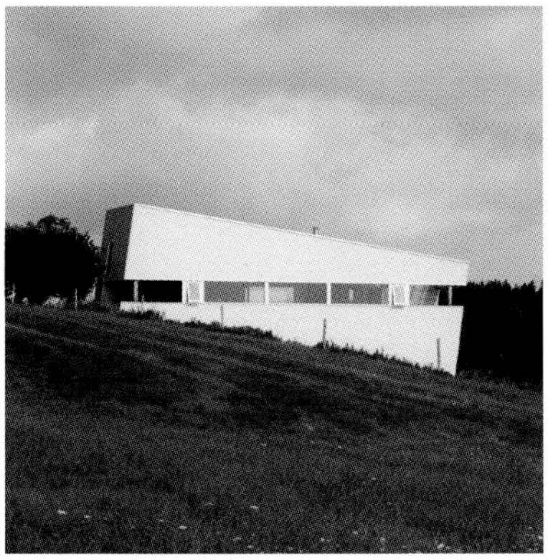

Day and Night Pavilions
Two Hulls House,
Nova Scotia, 2011

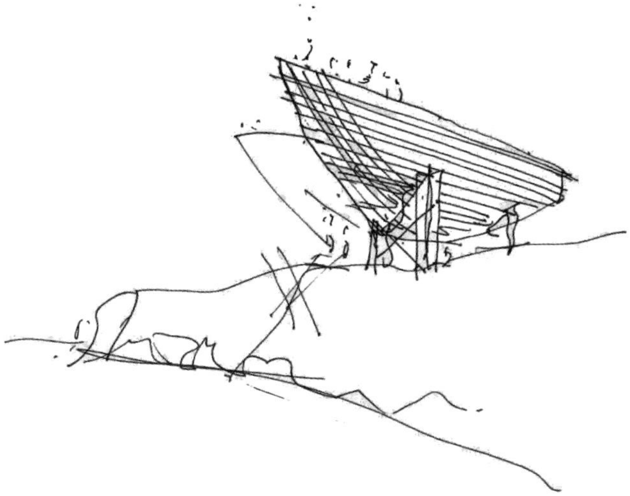

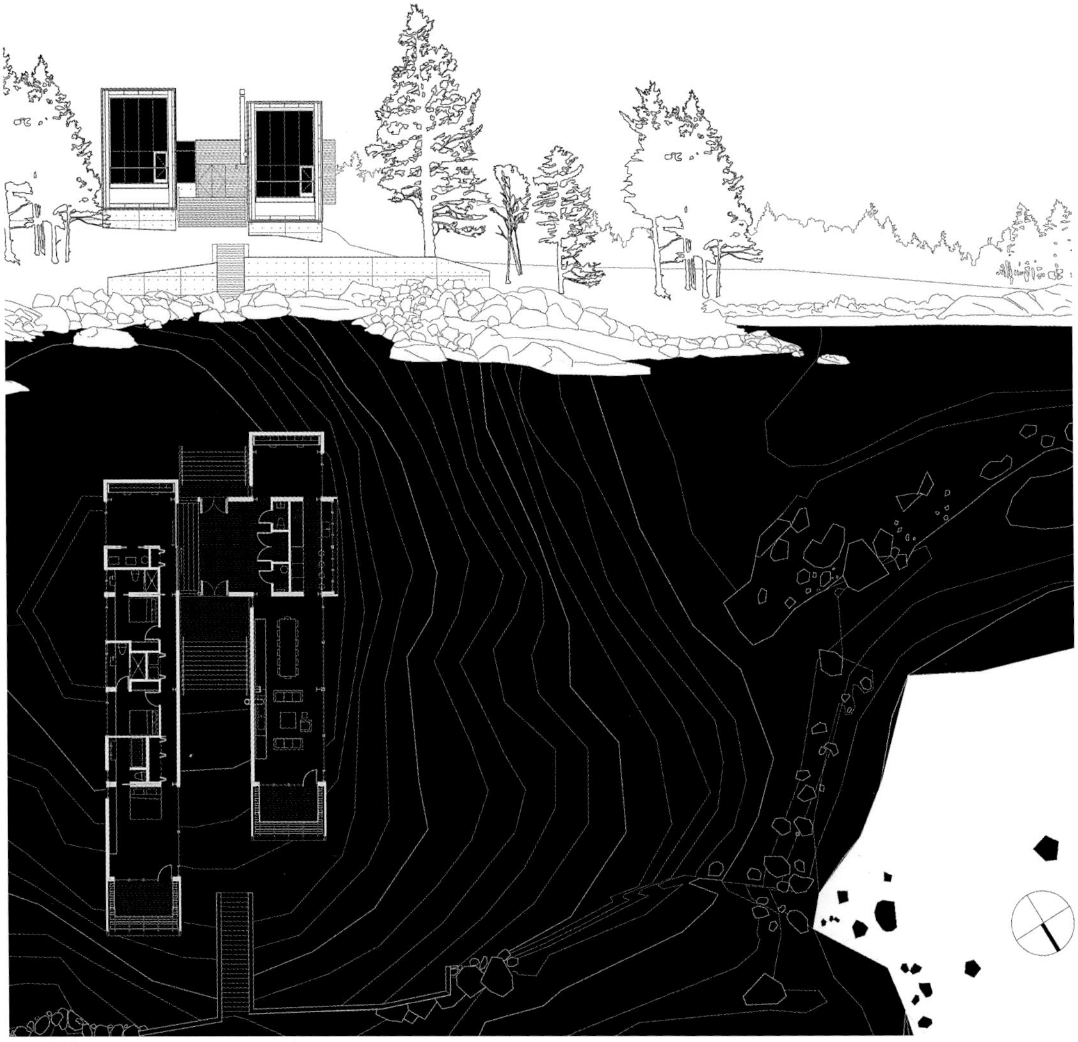

The Miller Hull Partnership

David Miller
Seattle, Washington, and
San Diego, California

Miller Hull is a firm whose work is grounded in the specific characteristics of their context in the Pacific Northwest. Their works all share a common set of ordering principles, yet they span from the domestic to the public scales—an increasingly rare achievement in today's world. At all scales, their work is remarkably consistent in both its quality and formal resolution, and reflects their deep understanding of the nature of their place. They "are interested in discovering the specific manifestations of a place," and their works are marked by the precision with which the experience of the inhabitants is engaged in the subtle fluctuations of climate, landscape, material, and light. Their work is at once a part of the modern tradition and an extension of the vernacular of the context in which they work. They believe that "architecture implies a constant rediscovery of dynamic human qualities translated into form and space," and they "strive to make a significant contribution to a richer modernism."

Domestic Roots
Roundy Residence,
Lopez Island, WA, 2010

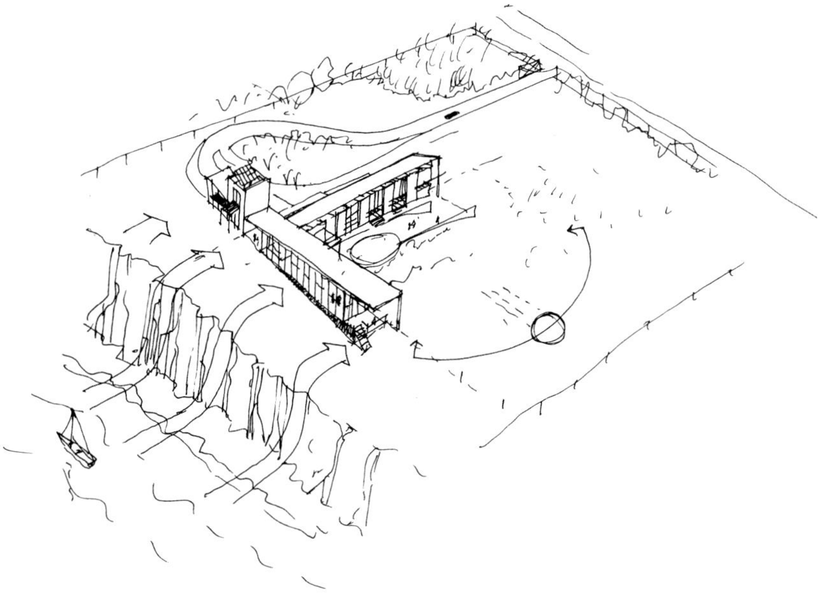

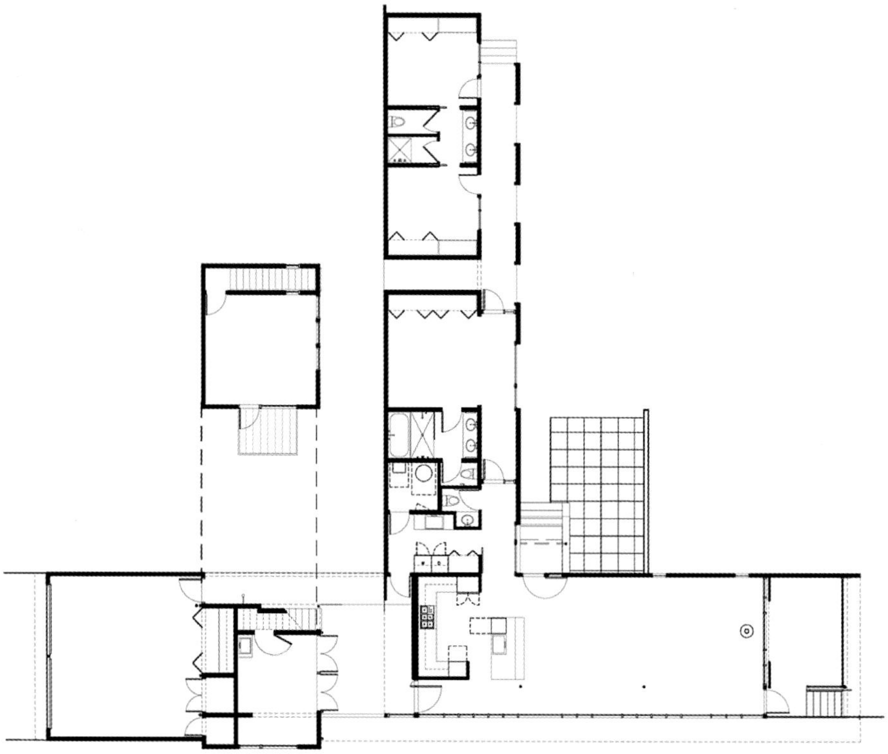

Glenn Murcutt

New South Wales, Australia

Glenn Murcutt is the world's leading practitioner of environmentally responsive architecture. In his work, climate and landscape are the primary generators of space and form. He believes that built works are, invariably, reflections of society's values, and that the house is central to architecture; "a house is an instrument played by nature." He draws inspiration from his intimate and extended interactions with nature, in both its general ordering principles and site-specific particularities. His work exemplifies those increasingly rare moments when craft springs from local culture, and as a result architecture is fully integrated into both its natural and social place. Murcutt believes that architecture involves an ethical responsibility to the people and place for which it is built. He seeks an architecture based on fundamental ordering principles learned through practice and shared with the architects of previous generations, and appropriately interpreted for its place. He states, "If we are to make an architecture that responds to our land, place, its climate, the flora, fauna, culture, technology, and time, then as architects we must work toward an architecture of response rather than an architecture of imposition."

Climate as form giver
Magney House,
Bingie Point, New South
Wales, Australia, 1982–84

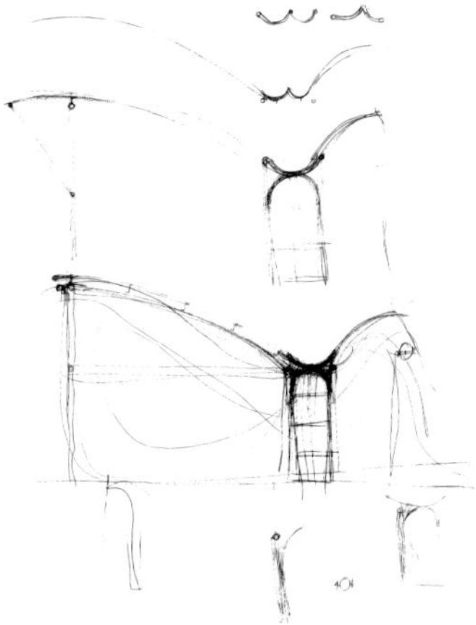

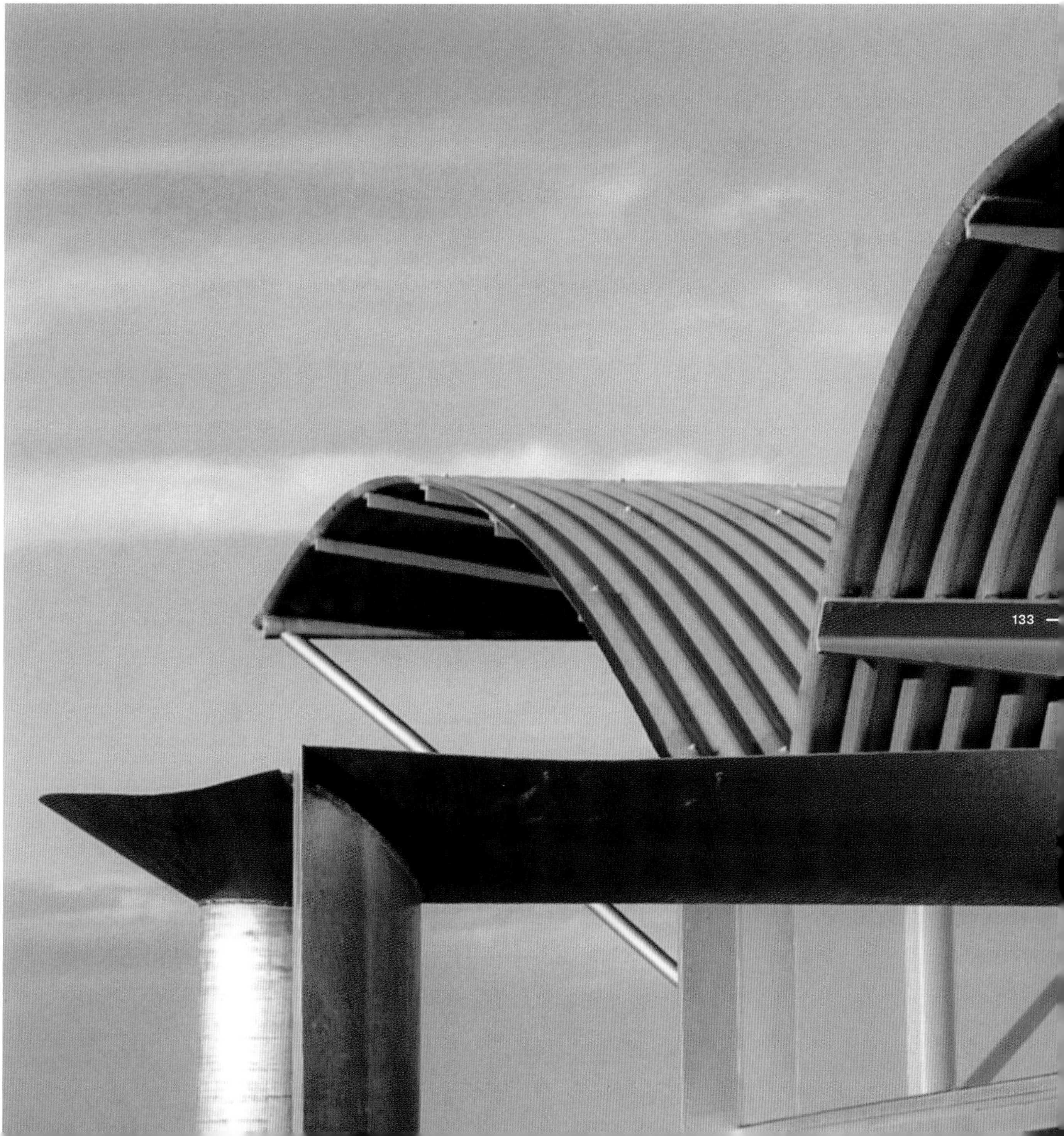

133

Unprecedented
Marie Short House,
Kempsey, New South
Wales, 1974–75

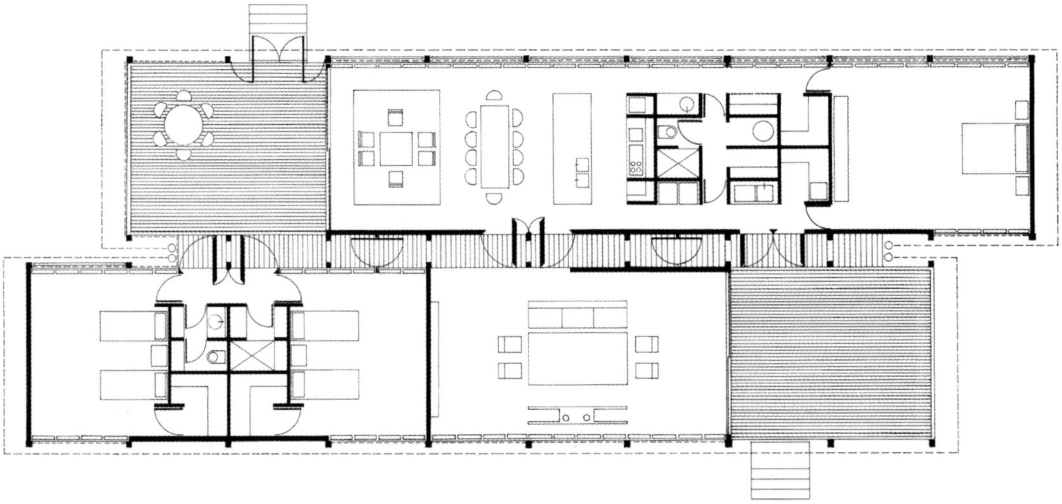

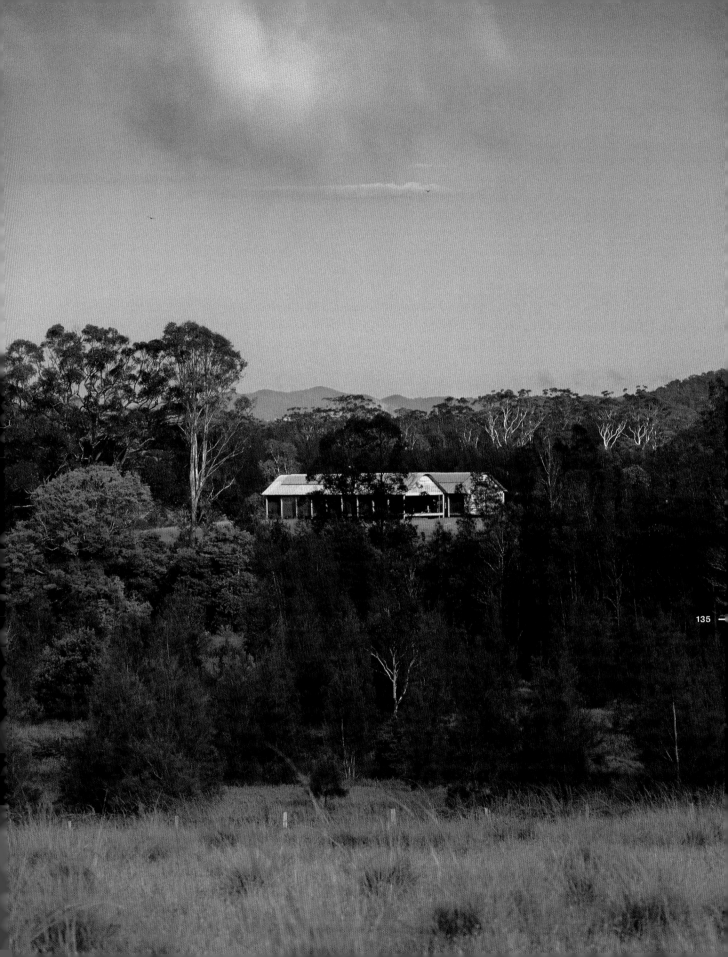

Enough Craft
Marika-Alderton House, Eastern Arnhem Land, Australia, 1991–94

Simpson Lee House, Mount Wilson, Blue Mountains, New South Wales, 1988–93

Next spread: Arthur and Yvonne Boyd Education Centre, Riversdale, New South Wales, 1996–99

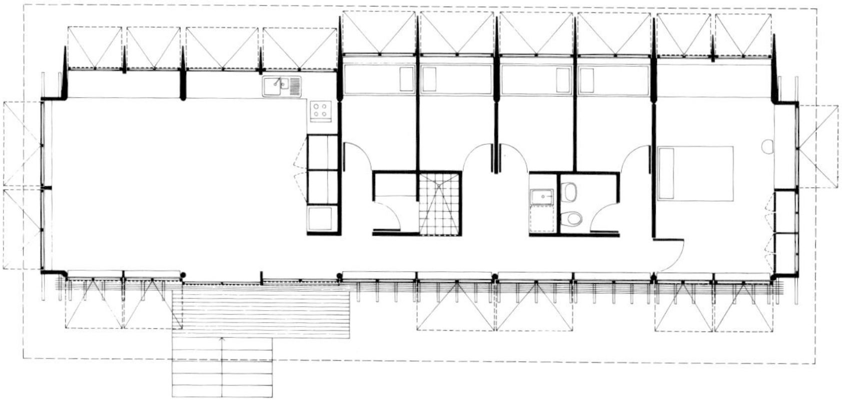

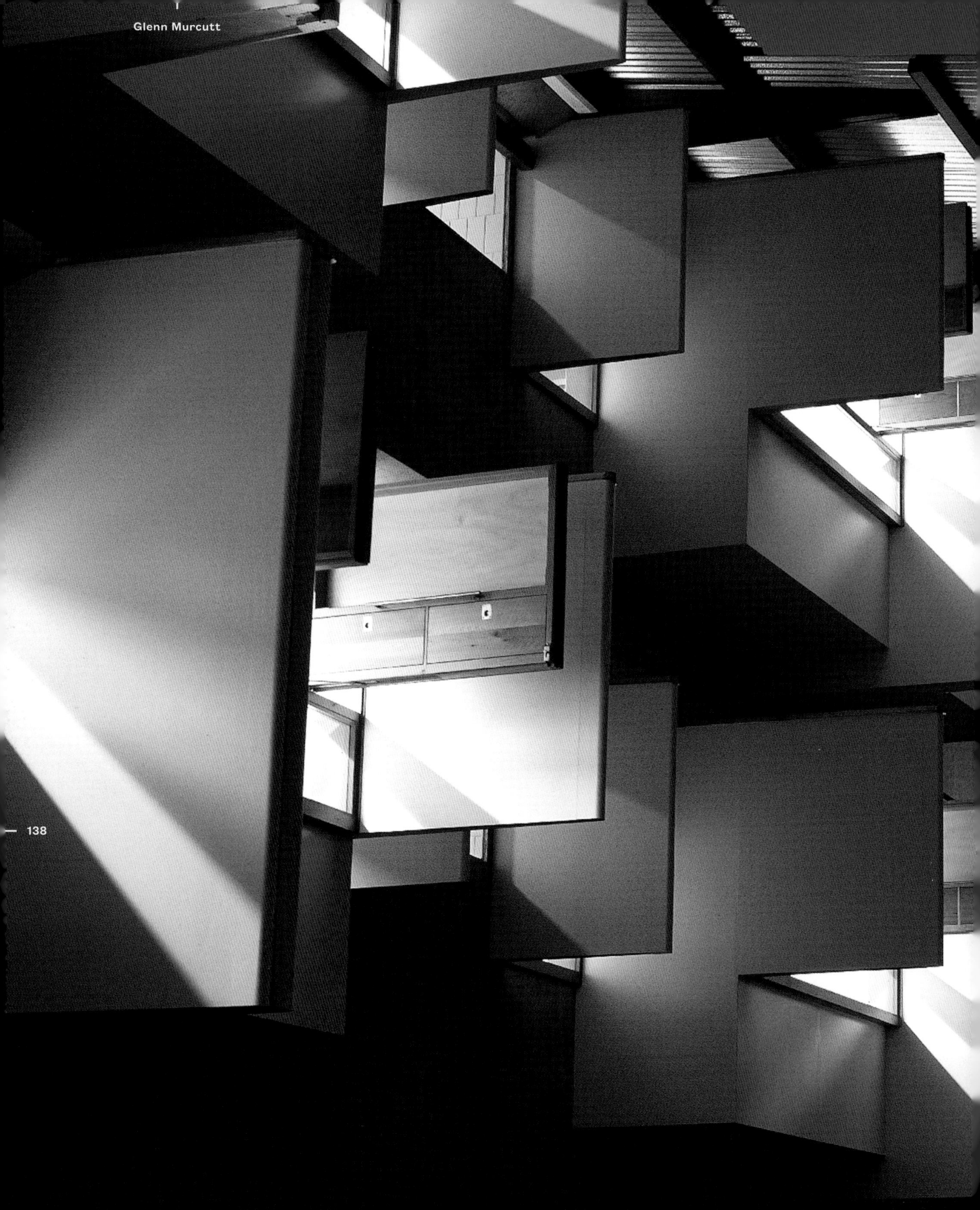

Patkau Architects

Patricia Patkau
Vancouver, British Columbia

Patricia Patkau sees her practice as increasingly focused on "constructing relations between things," as well as on the quality and craft of construction, and how these both affect the experience of inhabitation. Patkau Architects pursues "form finding," in the vein of Frei Otto, as opposed to form-making, seeking forms that arise from the construction of "binding relations between the places we inhabit and our desires and needs as communities and individuals." Their work, at both the domestic and public scales, is characterized by fitting itself into the situation, and they allow the design to emerge from "between the relationships and the material work." For the Patkaus, the environment is not the "setting" for inhabitation; rather the environment and the inhabitant are unified in the experience of place. Their work exhibits both formal skill and intellectual rigor, and they engage in pure research that often redirects the trajectory of their practice. Their design process engages "building as a form of knowing," and the works arise out of "a constant back and forth between construction and idea... with an attendant care and attention to the craft of the thing itself."

Dressmaking

Winnipeg Skating Shelters, Winnipeg, Manitoba, 2011

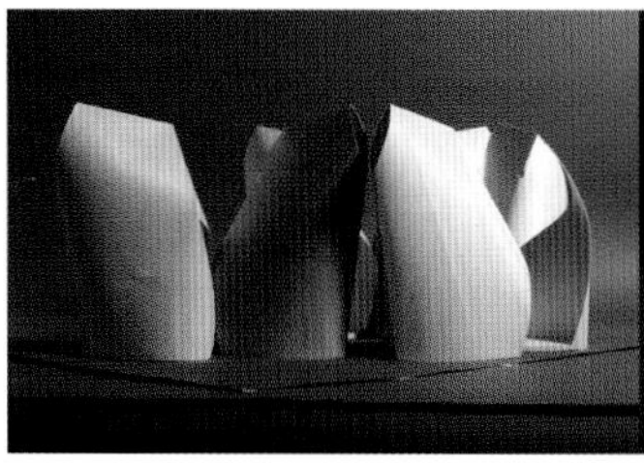

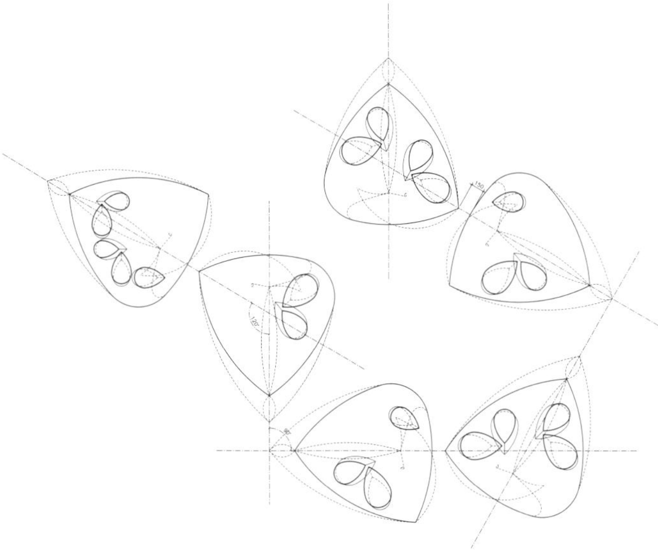

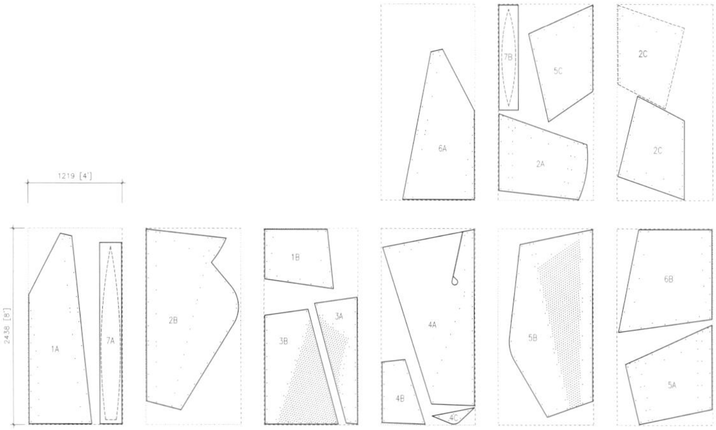

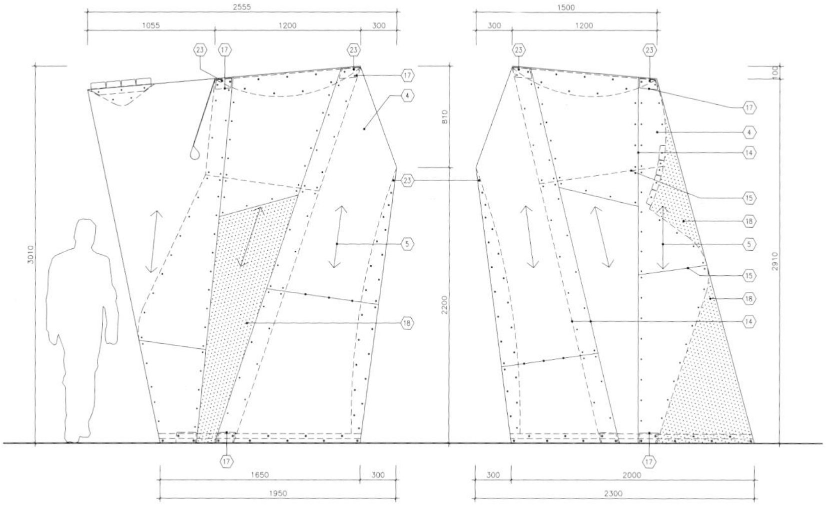
2555
1055
1200
300
1500
300
1200
3010
810
2200
2910
100
1650
300
1950
300
2000
2300

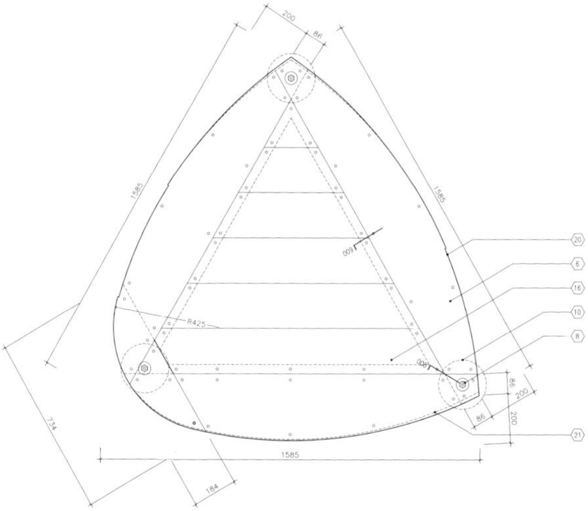
200
86
1585
1585
R425
734
184
1585
200
86
86
200

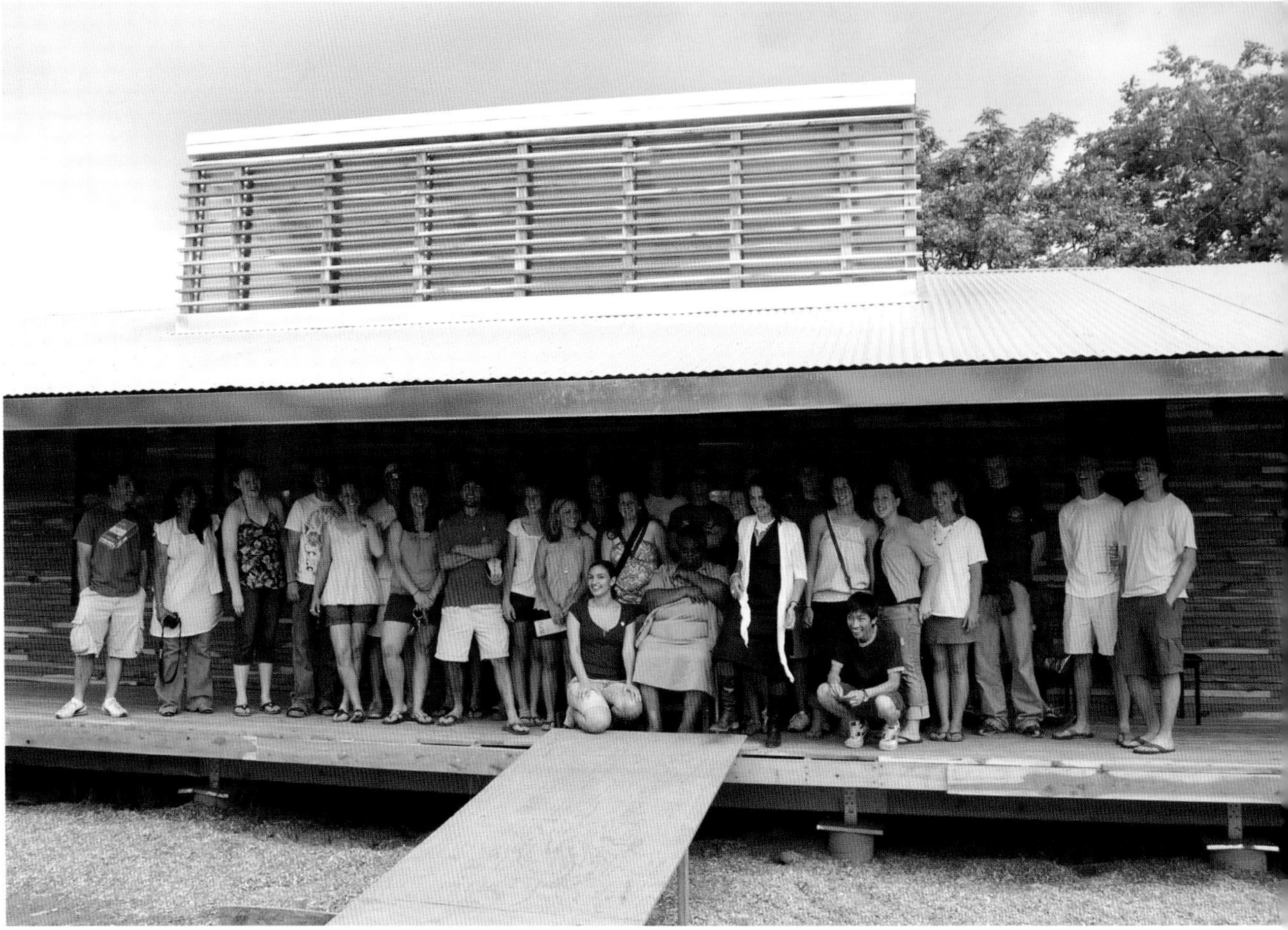

Rural Studio

Andrew Freear
Newbern, Alabama

Rural Studio, the visionary project begun by the late Samuel Mockbee, and continued today by Andrew Freear and his colleagues, may rightly be called the social conscience of our profession within the academic context. It operates as a model of both design-build education and disciplinary social engagement—"what we should do." Working in the poorest of places, the program remains committed to Mockbee's charge, in regards to everything they build, to "make it beautiful." The faculty and students are involved in building both public and private structures, all of which exemplify sustainable practices in that they reuse existing buildings or employ recycled materials. The program constructs one $20,000 house each year in an effort to address the needs of the hundreds of local citizens living below the poverty line. The Rural Studio exemplifies the belief that "people and place really do matter"; that architects must believe in the public realm; and that commitment to a place means accepting responsibility for the long-term health and welfare of that place and its people.

Monumental Modesty
Rose Lee's House,
Hale County, AL, 2009

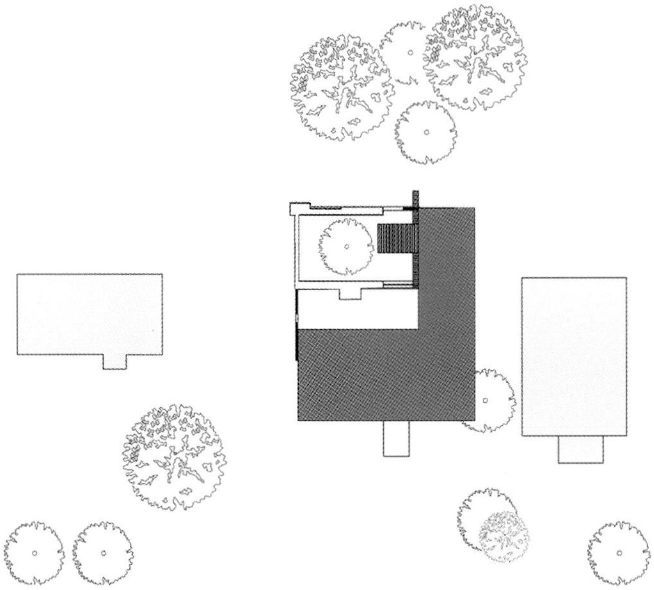

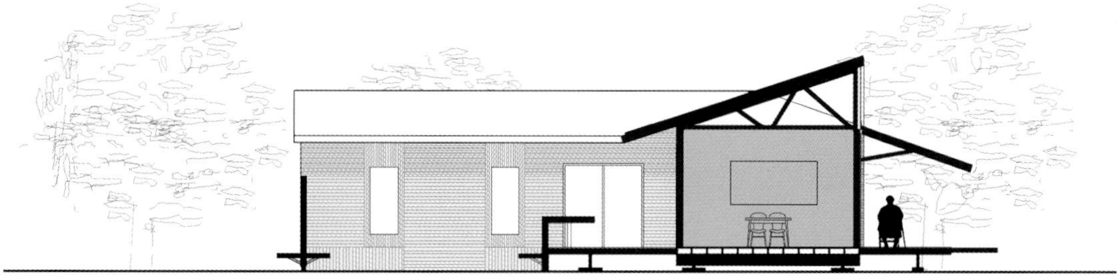

Shim-Sutcliffe Architects

Brigitte Shim
Toronto, Ontario

Brigitte Shim is deeply committed to realizing built works that engage the unique characteristics of the varied Canadian landscapes and foster the densification of urban centers through the development of alternative models to the suburb. Shim-Sutcliffe Architects begins each project by studying the context of each site and understanding the nature of the landscape or urban milieu, as well as learning from the way the place has been perceived and presented by artists. They see all their work, irrespective of scale, as a form of experimentation in the possibilities of architecture. In their work, they engage and expand the experiential qualities of light, landscape, nature, materials, and the variations of climate and seasons. Working in the ancient tradition of building craft as a carrier of cultural meaning, they construct modern works of unsurpassed craftsmanship, making architecture that celebrates each moment of human dwelling. In their works, light, material, and the unique qualities of place, whether urban or rural, are intertwined in an experience that enriches the rituals of daily life.

Sectional
Congregation Bet
Ha'am, South Portland,
ME, 2009

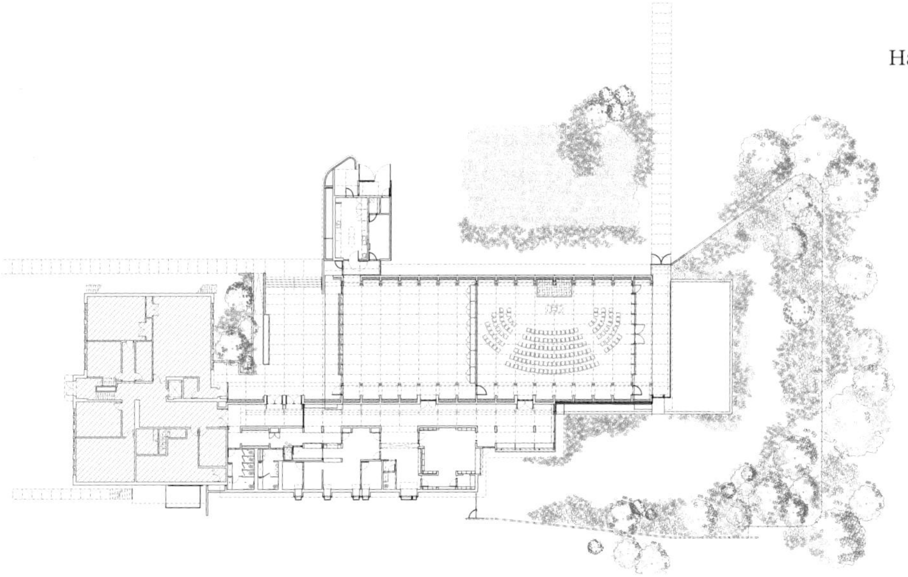

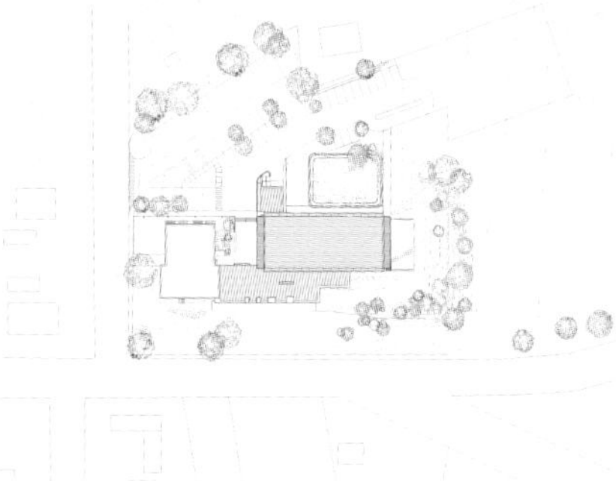

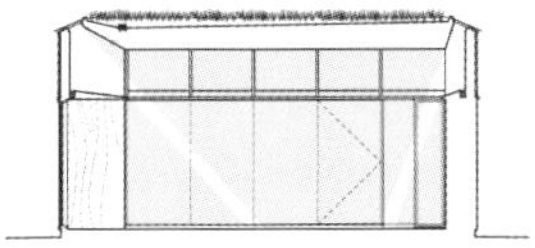

Dan Rockhill
Lawrence, Kansas

Studio 804

Studio 804, the design-build program that Dan Rockhill directs at the University of Kansas, has constructed a series of affordable houses and public commissions in Kansas. As a practicing architect, Rockhill was involved in the restoration of many historical building sites in Kansas, during which he analyzed and learned from the old building techniques. He emphasizes that the ultimate intention of Studio 804 is "to make the students better architects, not better builders." In this, the development of each individual's capacity for craft is essential, as is their engagement of traditional construction skills. The work of the studio is "tightly bound to the natural milieu and culture of the Kansas region. In the spirit of regionalism, the area's archetypal forms, Spartan aesthetics, frugal methods, and relationship to nature permeate the results." Rockhill leads by example; he maintains that universities, not the profession, should be the lead for engaging new technologies for realizing sustainable, affordable, and inventive buildings; and he believes that architecture can be sustainable and beautiful at the same time.

Modularity
Previous: Modular 3,
Kansas City, KS, 2006

This spread: Modular 1,
Kansas City, KS, 2004

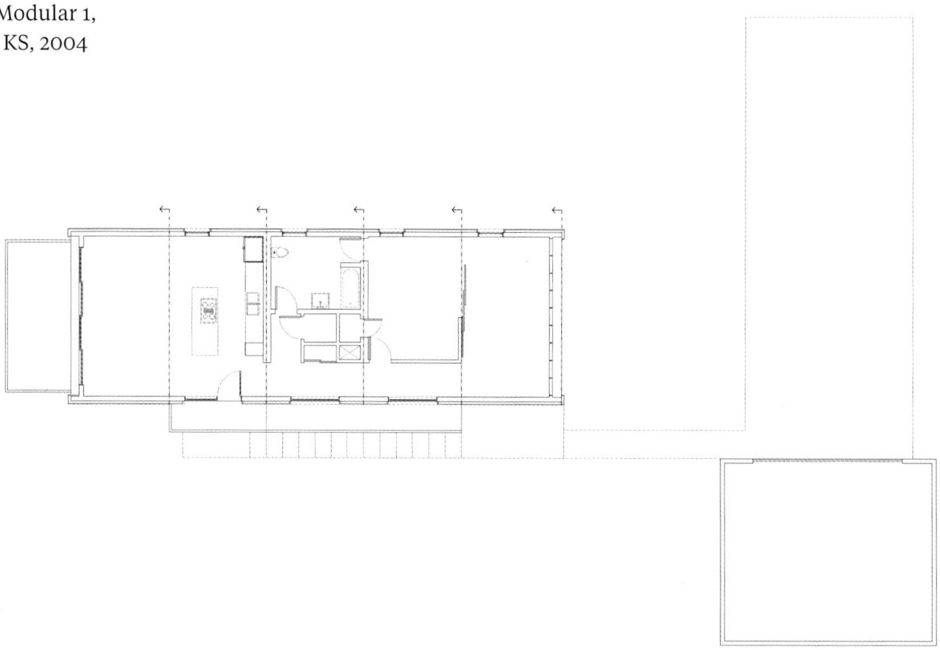

Springfield Street House,
Kansas City, KS, 2009

Prescott Passive House,
Kansas City, KS, 2010

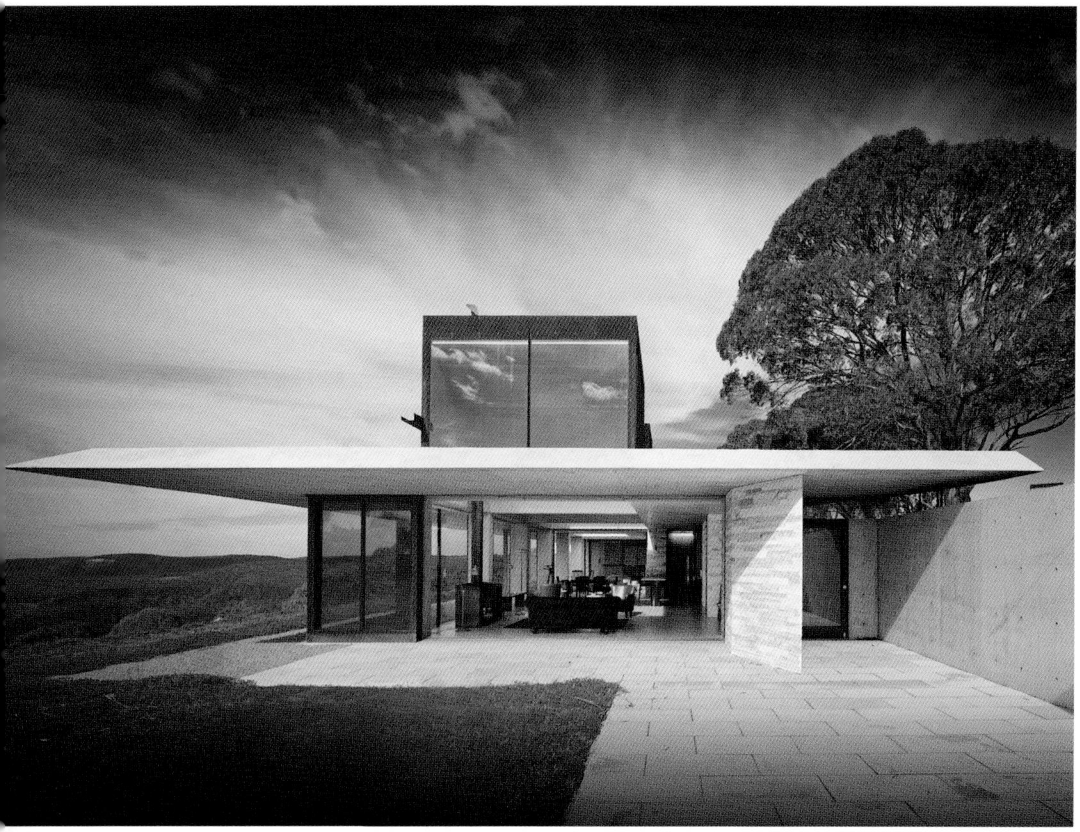

Peter Stutchbury
Newport, Australia

Peter Stutchbury Architecture

Stutchbury's architecture comes out of a deep respect for and understanding of his place in Australia and its land, climate, material culture, and indigenous building traditions. He believes that an embedded environmental sensitivity and placemaking are both part of our inherent makeup, and that we are capable of reading the landscape, reading the way animals build their dwellings, and reading the way aboriginal humans built their dwellings. In his work, Stutchbury emphasizes space and light, connection to landscape, structural clarity, and construction of a mood—a sense of serenity for the inhabitants. Working within the widely varied climates of Australia, his works attain a remarkable level of sustainability while deploying the most typical of industrial and agricultural construction materials and methods. In designing, he "does not seek to produce a gesture, but rather to study the surroundings, both immediate and distant." His works are intended as "an interpretation of all the factors that accumulate to form a story of belonging to a place." As a result, his architecture has a minimal presence formally, yet it allows a maximal experience spatially and materially.

Aboriginal Ethic
Invisible House, Blue Mountains, New South Wales, Australia, 2010

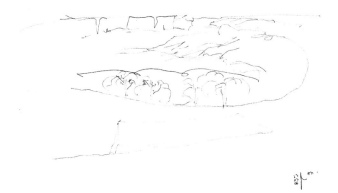

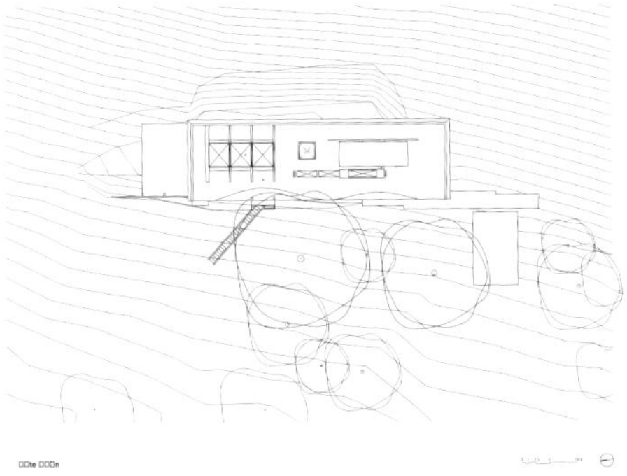

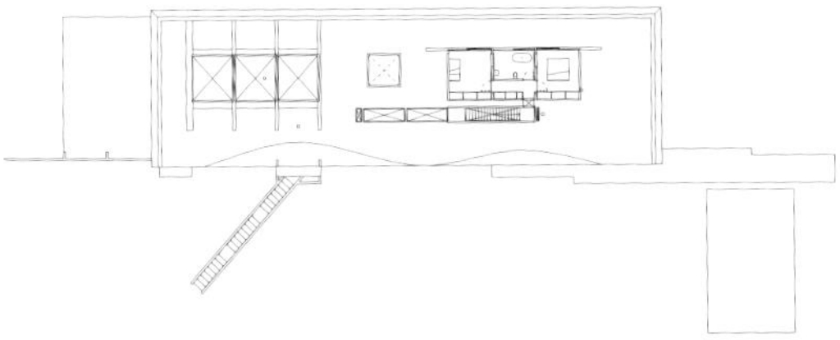

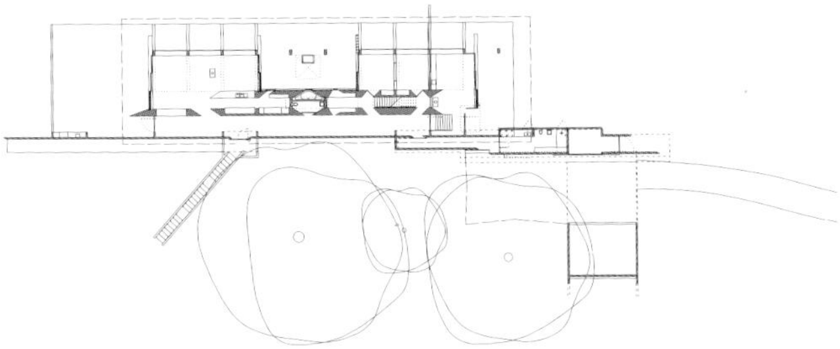

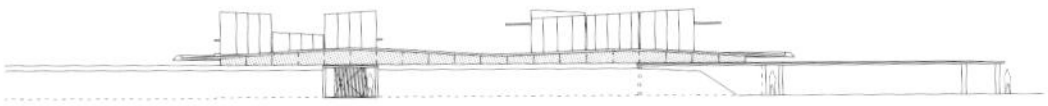

Vincent James and Jennifer Yoos
Minneapolis, Minnesota

VJAA

The work of Vincent James and Jennifer Yoos has evolved toward the goal of being a "polyvalent," "reflexive practice," one that is capable of deploying a diverse set of conceptual and material responses to the unique qualities of program and place. VJAA's work exhibits a level of formal and material precision and minimalism that results in an increased density and richness of experience for the inhabitants; "The hallucinatory effect derives from the extraordinary clarity and not from mystery or mist. Nothing is more fantastic, ultimately, than precision." They are critical of formal style and material uniformity, and, rather than seeking to propagate an image, they develop each project as an organic idea specific to its site. Arguing that eccentricity acts to curtail disciplinary discourse, their work engages the modern tradition of typological evolution. Their "reflexive practice" involves engaging the context, environment, and traditions of building, integrating these with the local culture and social practices of the inhabitants. All their work actively reengages existing local craft and material traditions in order to allow them to be adapted for new uses and to be regrounded in our time.

Memory of Place
Charles Hostler
Student Center, Beirut,
Lebanon, 2008

KOURA
KOURA

ESSAYS

Constructing and Caring for Place

Robert McCarter

Brian MacKay-Lyons and Juhani Pallasmaa look over the boathouse.

Whatever space and time mean, place and occasion mean more. For space in the image of man is place, and time in the image of man is occasion.
—Aldo van Eyck, 1960[1]

We gathered in a place of distinct qualities and character, a remote, windswept, and fog-bound peninsular coast on the northeast edge of the continent, coming together to think about the way in which, for architects and poets alike, ideas only exist in things. The gathering of leading international practitioners and critics, sharing their works, thoughts, and aspirations for architecture, took place within a set of carefully constructed buildings, woven over and among the foundations of an ancient village—a place known to the participants as "Ghost." The discussions, reactions, and insights arising from the meeting of peers of a uniformly high caliber, along with the positive reinforcement of their individual trajectories, will no doubt prove to be the most constructive outcome of this event, and the source of its lasting influence. These collegial and constructive dialogues among disciplinary peers bring to mind the only real precedents for such meetings in the modern period—the International Congress of Modern Architecture (CIAM), starting in 1928, and the Team 10 group that emerged from CIAM in the 1950s. It is worth noting that the meetings of CIAM and Team 10 are most often remembered today by the names of the places where they gathered—Athens, Dubrovnik, Otterlo, Royaumont.

The Ghost 13: Ideas in Things symposium began by revisiting the concept of "critical regionalism," originally defined in the early 1980s by Alexander Tzonis, Liane Lefaivre, and Kenneth Frampton and understood as a shared characteristic of the work being presented. In addition to being defined as a constructively critical continuation of modern architecture, critical regionalism also addresses how to see and respond appropriately to a particular place. As Harwell Hamilton Harris noted in 1954, what he called "restrictive regionalism" closes itself off from the outside world and contemporary developments, while "liberative regionalism" engages ideas coming from the outside world and thereby is not restricted by its place, either in the limitations of the place or in the potential reach of the work's implications.[2] This concept of regionalism, and its relation to contemporary global developments, is paralleled by that proposed in 1961 by Paul Ricoeur, who noted the dichotomous relation between what he called "local culture"—the grounded character of places that allows them to be the source of our identity—and "universal civilization"—the technical and material benefits of modernization that all of mankind, irrespective of location, wish to receive. "There is the paradox: how to become modern and to return to sources," as Ricoeur noted, and this paradox pivots around the relation between the historical form of a place and the modern intervention within it; "The problem is not simply to repeat the past, but rather to take root in it in order to ceaselessly invent."[3]

The symposium participants all share the characteristics of being contemporary critical practitioners, engaging emerging ideas and ways of making from around the world, as well as being from places that have shaped their character and their work. As a paradoxical result of their grounding of universal conceptions in local material cultures, the work of these architects has had significant impact on the larger, global context. These architects share an acute sensitivity to place, rural and urban. Their empathic engagement of the context has resulted in designs that are at once *responsive* and *responsible*—responsive to existing material culture, both agricultural and urban, and to patterns of previous inhabitation of each place in which they work; responsible in that they pursue a minimal intervention that nevertheless results in maximal experiential enrichment.

Another shared attribute of the assembled architects is their eagerness to engage not only the work of their contemporaries, but also the works of the generations of practitioners who went before them—Frank Lloyd Wright was mentioned on more than one occasion during the symposium. As part of what we might call "the tradition of practice," their works, despite being richly diverse, are invariably characterized by a combination of the *practical* and the *poetic*. The practical engages those aspects of appropriateness, functional suitability, limited use of energy and resources, proper solar orientation, and local material culture, all learned from the vernacular of a place—as Brian MacKay-Lyons has said, "what you make when you cannot afford to make mistakes." On the other hand, the poetic involves the efforts to enrich the experience of the inhabitants through the engagement of local climate, context, and culture, understanding that architecture is where life quite literally *takes place*. With surprising modesty, Wright said that architecture was the "background or framework" for the rituals of daily life, and at the time of his statement, the beginning of the twentieth century, only the poetic qualities of an architect's work were considered worth noting.[4] This was so because, for those engaged in the tradition of practice, the practical aspects of architectural practice were considered the minimum definition of professional competence, and thus not worth mentioning; if one did not take care of the practical matters in one's first design, one would not receive a second commission. The tradition of practice, which we have inherited from architects such as Wright, is an integrated, synthetic fusion of the poetic and the practical.

Yet today we have witnessed the rise of the "specialist" practice, which addresses only a small portion of the traditional definition of architecture. This subdivision of the discipline has led to firms that advertise their specialization in a few practical capacities of often-dubious value (such as the ubiquitous LEED certification, to name only the most egregious). Such a limited definition of professional expertise in architecture would not have been considered even minimally competent in Wright's time, one hundred years ago—why is it that we are willing and indeed eager to accept it today? An architecture that considers *placemaking* to be its primary task could never be so narrowly defined, and the work of the architects who gathered in Nova Scotia collectively suggests an opposite approach to the definition of the task of architecture. In this integrated way of working, the appropriate response to a very particular context—where the architect "learned to see the place," as Wendell Burnette said at Ghost 13—is not limited in its implications to that specific place, but in fact has far wider import.

In a similar way, the symposium provided the grounds and opportunity for a far broader discussion of the state of architecture and architectural education today. In this, it could be argued that it is precisely the three thematic anchors of the symposium—*place*, *craft*, and *community* (or the public realm)—that are most at risk of disappearing from the world. These three concepts are also joined in the definition of "critical practice" that characterizes the symposium participants and their fellow travelers. Here I am engaging Kenneth Frampton's recent definition of critical practice as inherently involving *constructing* and *caring* for place:

> In the ninety years that have elapsed since the first utopian gestures of the Futurist avant-garde, radical modernism has become increasingly distanced from the life-world through the aestheticization of form, so that today little remains of the revolutionary potential of the original modern movement. From this standpoint, we may even think of the modern project as the lost cause of the welfare state; one that may now only be redeemed on an ad hoc basis through the self-conscious generation of a critical practice; one which construes every commission as the occasion for the creation and maintenance of place.[5]

While craft is required to construct place, Hannah Arendt pointed out in 1958 that place is required in order for the public realm to come into existence.[6] Architects take the lead in the construction of the place that houses the public realm, yet the community is essential to the caring for and maintenance of that place. This brings to mind the more integrated definition of placemaking given in 1960 by Aldo van Eyck, developed in his discussions with his fellow members of Team 10 as they searched for an experiential definition of modern architecture—an alternative to the abstractions of Sigfried Giedion's *space* and *time*, and a definition that appears as the epigraph to this essay.

This definition of place and its relation to architectural practice is grounded in the daily experience of the inhabitants and suggests, as David Chipperfield wrote in 1994, that any theory as to the nature of architecture should be generated from practice, and not the other way around.[7] In editing a history of architectural education in America, Joan Ockman found that the separation of theory from practice in academia reached its most extreme point during the late 1990s, leading to what she called "the exhaustion of theory" in architectural education, which was followed by a renewed emphasis on practice beginning around 2000.[8] It was around that time that the dean of a prominent Ivy League school of architecture told the faculty that they would need to choose either thinking or making—and given that, in his definition, academia was the province of thinking, they should leave making to the practitioners. Standing directly opposite this disintegrative reasoning is Richard Sennett, who noted that his first thought regarding his book, *The Craftsman*, was that "making is thinking."[9]

A pair of primary themes emerged in the discussions at the symposium, the first being the relation between critical practice and place, and the second being the relation between ideas and the things we make that form those places—the fusion of thinking and making understood as "the thought of construction," to use Sverre Fehn's apt phrase. Giambattista Vico, the early eighteenth-century philosopher, held that mankind's history is quite literally embodied in what we have made. Vico's aphorism, *verum ipsum factum*, "truth is in the made," could have served as a motto for the architects gathered in the eighteenth-century barn on the Nova Scotia coast. Upon his appointment as dean of IUAV, the school of architecture in Venice, Carlo Scarpa took Vico's *verum ipsum factum* as the motto of the school, to be inscribed on the diplomas and carved over the entry gate he designed. Translated by Scarpa as "we only know what we make," this thought embodied in construction precisely defines Scarpa's understanding of both the education and working method of an architect, where thinking and making, "construing and constructing" (to use Marco Frascari's telling phrase), are irrevocably joined in the enacting of a work of architecture.[10] Today we need a renewed commitment to this understanding as a way of counteracting the contemporary bias toward thinking *without* making, and making *without* thinking, both of which tend to dominate architectural education and theoretical discourse.

Here it would perhaps be helpful to introduce a distinction recently made by David Van Zanten in framing the differences in modes of practice between Louis Sullivan, Frank Lloyd Wright, and Louis Kahn and their respective contemporary practitioners of the globalized styles of École des Beaux-Arts classicism and mid-twentieth-century International Style modernism. Van Zanten notes that the method taught at the École des Beaux-Arts, and paralleled by the later International Style of modernism, was in fact not a design process at all, but rather a predetermined compositional procedure, an "art of command" where the architect dictates the form of the building, based on preconceived models, and both the place for which it is intended and the materials out of which it is made have no effect on the design—a separation of thinking and making. On the other hand, Van Zanten argues that Sullivan, Wright, and Kahn practiced what he calls the "art of nurture," a process of design where the architect seeks an appropriate fit between function and form, fitting the spatial geometry to the pattern of human activity, and where both the place in which the structure is built and the nature of the materials with which it is made have significant effect on the design—an integration of thinking and making.[11] Weaving metaphors abound in this conception of design as *nurture* and *fit*, and the work of the architects assembled for the symposium may similarly be characterized as a *weaving* of enclosures that make interiors of both outside and inside space, as opposed to the *sculpting* of freestanding objects. Also implicit in this conception is design defined as *doing what is appropriate*— the only thing Kahn thought he could teach his students.

As a way of counteracting the accelerating tendency for architecture, through the various ways in which it is publicized today, to be reinterpreted as yet another expression of ever-changing fashion, we should remember that Alvar Aalto pointed in exactly the opposite direction when he said that what matters in architecture is not what a building looks like the day it opens, but what it is like to live in thirty years later. In speaking of what a building is like to live in, Aalto articulated a concept of what we would today call sustainability, one that recognizes that the most sustainable buildings are not only those that are most efficient in technical and economical terms, but those that sustain life—those that people want to live in, thirty years after they are built. Truly sustainable architecture involves the three themes of the symposium—place, craft, and community—and both culture and ecology are involved in the construction of place. Truly sustainable architecture of this type is also never simply the result of building industry–determined technical formulas but, instead, as a fundamental act of placemaking, always involves criticality and resistance. Place is intimately bound with making, and place should be understood as the most important thing we make. The symposium theme of "ideas in things," unfolded in the making of place, craft, and community, finds resonance in Peter Zumthor's recent statement, "There are no ideas except in things"—a close rephrasing of a line from a poem by William Carlos Williams.[12] As a cautionary closing note for a symposium on architecture, where words are employed to communicate ideas among those who make things, the last word should go to Ralph Waldo Emerson: "No answer in words can reply to a question of things."[13]

1 Vincent Ligtelijn and Francis Strauven, eds., Aldo van Eyck: *Writings, Vol. 2* (Amsterdam: SUN, 2008), 293.

2 Harwell Hamilton Harris, "Regionalism and Nationalism in Architecture," *Texas Quarterly* (February 1958): 58.

3 Paul Ricoeur, "Civilization and National Cultures," in *History and Truth* (Evanston: Northwestern University Press, 1965), 277, 282.

4 Frank Lloyd Wright, "Architect, Architecture and the Client," in *Frank Lloyd Wright Collected Writings, Vol. 1* (New York: Rizzoli, 1992), 36.

5 Kenneth Frampton, *The Evolution of 20th Century Architecture: A Synoptic Account* (Vienna: Springer, 2007), 145.

6 Hannah Arendt, *The Human Condition* (Chicago: University of Chicago Press, 1958), 49.

7 David Chipperfield, *Theoretical Practice* (London: Artemis London Ltd., 1994).

8 Joan Ockman, in a talk given at Washington University, April 2, 2011.

9 Richard Sennett, *The Craftsman* (New Haven, CT: Yale University Press, 2008), ix.

10 Marco Frascari, "The Tell-the-Tale Detail," *VIA 7: The Building of Architecture* (1984): 24.

11 David Van Zanten, "Kahn and Architectural Composition," unpublished paper read on January 24, 2004, at the conference "The Legacy of Louis I. Kahn," Yale University; courtesy of the author.

12 Peter Zumthor, quoted in Michael Kimmelman, The Ascension of Peter Zumthor," the *New York Times Sunday Magazine* (March 2011).

13 Ralph Waldo Emerson, "The Over-Soul" (1841), *Ralph Waldo Emerson: Essays and Lectures*, ed. Joel Porte (New York: Library of America, 1983), 394.

Construction and Composition, Concept Versus Craft

Peter Buchanan

Peter Buchanan speaks about craft in architecture.

Craft was the theme of the second day of Ghost 13, sandwiched between Place and Community. Before focusing on craft, it is worth briefly exploring why Brian MacKay-Lyons might have chosen this particular trinity. What links place, craft, and community, beyond their obvious centrality in MacKay-Lyons's own life and work?

With the waning of the simple certainties of modern architecture, and after the anything-goes pluralism of postmodernity, architecture in general, as opposed to that represented at Ghost 13, has rather lost its bearings and seems ungrounded, without a sense of larger purpose or context. Ultimately this derives from modernity's overly exclusive emphasis on the objective, the realm of scientific materialism, at the expense of the subjective, particularly culture. Among other things, this led to modern architecture's reduction of human occupation to function, our actions as understood by detached observation, rather than considered as dwelling or habitation, words resonant with subjectivity.

Thus a modern building is a functional device, Le Corbusier's *machine à habiter*, subservient to the user, of value only when used and obsolete afterward. This is very different from premodern buildings, which are cultural artifacts that are mediators (thus more elevated in status than mere functional devices) between us and the world, both natural and manmade. The rhetorical devices and ornament rejected by modernism connect us with the long march of history and our ancestors, with myths of origins and so on, while also addressing the future and our descendants. They thus embed the building and its occupants in local culture as well as in much larger temporal and spatial contexts than does modernity's fixation with the short term and disinterest in context. (Postmodernity might have rekindled an interest in context, but its engagement with culture remains superficial.) Modernity's reductionism inevitably leads to the creation of autistic buildings shaped only around their internal workings and to the dismissal of larger impacts on the environment as mere externalities—hence the destructiveness of modernity and modern architecture. This is why we have no chance of advancing to sustainability without reappraising the role of culture and starting the long process of regenerating it.

As with critical regionalism—a theme introduced by Kenneth Frampton on the first night and in the air throughout Ghost 13—place, craft, and community all refer to something local and preexisting and so embrace a larger spatiotemporal realm than typifies modernity. Place is axiomatically local and long preexists the architect's transformation of it; place also extends far beyond the confines of the site. All crafts have long traditions, including an expertise with local materials, as well as specific tools and ways of working. Like place, these traditions need to be respected, even when introducing innovations. Community too is local and usually preexists the architect's involvement; even if it does not, it is something forged slowly in the long term.

Place, craft, and community are all intrinsic to culture, which is local, imbued with traditions of making, and sustained by communal narratives that vivify place and craft practices. As with culture, these are all intrinsic to how we create ourselves and acquire depth and meaning. Place is intrinsic to identity, as are craft and community: patient craftsmanship shapes who you are and contributes to the formation of true character; community is essential to self-knowledge—you only know yourself to the degree you are fully known by others. Thus attention to Ghost 13's organizing trinity is required for a fully embedded architecture to which people can relate in depth.

Having set this context, let's narrow our discussion to craft, although in a broader sense than many architects understand it and than MacKay-Lyons probably intended.

Many, if not most, architects associate craft with the construction and detailing of buildings, with the handling of materials and the way materials are brought together—with what some may see as the realm of the artisan. Important as these are, this is much too narrow a notion of craft, which pertains to all aspects of architecture. The composition of a building is crafted—the external massing as well as the disposition of and flow between its spaces. Hence the plan in particular is honed until its logic and life can be gleaned at a glance. Often, too, elevations are drawn and redrawn until they combine, say, a certain vivacity with an easy repose. It is within this larger context that the narrower notion of craft then finds its true place, perhaps unifying the design and making it more legible. Some successful architects, as part of what ensures success, also craft the narratives of their lives. This gives them and their works deep roots in such things as personal and family history, in the locality and its past, as well as an empowering trajectory into the future. And more than a few architects self-consciously craft their public personas.

So what is craft? It is a skill at working with a particular medium over which mastery is gained through patient, repetitive practice. Because both parts of this definition are crucial to any proper understanding of craft, they bear repeating and expanding: craft entails working in a particular medium, which has its own characteristics to be understood and respected; the crucial feeling for and mastery of that medium is only arrived at through patient repetition, closely attentive to those characteristics.

There are a multitude of mediums in which craftsmen work. These range from physical materials such as the clay, wood, leather, wool, and various metals typically associated with crafts (the products found in craft shops) to physically intangible words (in prose, poetry, plays, scripts for film and television, and physical performance in reading and acting), music (both composition and performance), and software and computer games. In architecture such media include, among many others, form and space and light and structure; the choreography of circulation, building materials, components, and joints; and the diverse processes of on-site assembly.

More important than defining and listing these mediums, both difficult tasks, is to understand that they take time to explore and master. The long process of acquiring mastery brings benefits beyond a mere capacity for virtuosity that, if showy or intrusive, is probably a betrayal of the spirit of craftsmanship. The gradual refinement of skill, the dexterity in manipulating the medium, not only develops that crucial deep feeling for the medium but also the discrimination on which sure aesthetic judgment is founded. With constant repetition and practice, the skill, along with the innate knowledge and intuitive discernment it brings, becomes embodied or unconscious knowledge, so that it can be applied to the highest of standards almost without conscious thought.[1]

All experienced designers must be familiar with the phenomenon of “thinking with the fingers.” You have finished a design and are happy with it; the plan looks pretty much perfect. Then you start to loosely resketch it, the fingers retracing the form virtually without thought—and almost without noticing it they depart from what had seemed the final plan, easing a corner, altering an angle, clarifying a latent but unnoticed visual echo. The rough sketches of Alvar Aalto, with their tentative shaky lines from a soft pencil, lightly held and barely guided, illustrate this process vividly. Suddenly the plan has a new sense of flow and life, of coherence and wholeness. Then the conscious mind kicks in, to ponder the improvement and how it was achieved, and to consider whether it might be taken further. This results in the steady advance characteristic of mastering a craft and crafting a design, which brings together head and hand, conscious mind and intuition.

Once a craft is mastered, of course—after, in today's familiar term, investing ten thousand hours—it is not necessary to constantly revise and refine each work. Instead you draw on your accumulated skill and powers of discernment as an instantly available, almost unconscious, embodied knowledge. Thus jazz musicians, after years of practice (or "woodshedding," as they refer to it), can spontaneously improvise. And Frank Lloyd Wright could speedily conjure a seemingly endless sequence of masterful new designs—"shaking them out of my sleeve," as he claimed. Pablo Picasso, too, could knock out several drawings and a couple of paintings on the same day, each of a visceral intensity that comes from precision of concept and color mixed with the spontaneity of speedy brushwork, all mastered through years of playful work. Another consequence of this mastery, which probably most architects have witnessed, is the ability of an experienced designer to just glance at someone else's plan and see that something is wrong or unresolved. Or, equally quickly, to see that decreasing or enlarging the sizing and spacing of rafters, say, would both animate and better integrate a design.

One mark of a well-crafted work is an air of inevitability or "rightness": it might be highly inventive and original, yet it never looks overly contrived. So crafting a design is a process of distillation and synthesis as much as of elaboration, of eliminating the inessential and so burnishing an understated and enlivening richness. It also involves knowing when to stop, whether elaborating or refining. Some buildings take the quest for precision too far—particularly of construction and detail, but also of overly prescriptive planning—and tip over into preciousness or a life-sapping perfectionism. It is instructive to notice that some of the most lovely and moving works from the past, such as humble vernacular buildings, acquire some of their vivacity from irregularities and imperfections. From this patient, iterative design process, the resulting building acquires crucial qualities that, by appealing to more than the eye and the conscious mind, engage the user over the long term at some deep, if subliminal, level. This is because in this process of honing, the whole designer—including the body, instinctual reflexes, and the unconscious depths that constitute most of the mind—becomes invested in both the process and the final work. In turn this evokes some recognition and response, often only at an unconscious level, in the whole of the person who encounters the work.

Much current art and architecture elevate concept over craft, whether as conceptual art or postmodern architecture. The latter is most illuminatingly understood as illustrating (representing, in the jargon) some theory or concept. (The notion that historic "quotes" produce populist architecture is only one such theory.) But just as conceptual art cannot hold the attention beyond the time it takes to "get" the idea, neither can theory-driven or "critical" architecture ungrounded in the mastery of craft elicit a rewarding long-term engagement. Too often, elevating concept over craft results in a lack of interest in both materiality and construction (thus many postmodern works, such as the early houses of Michael Graves and Peter Eisenman, are made of crud—Sheetrock) and in working through a design to where it enriches prolonged familiarity. Theory and concept, even those much less spurious than those entertained by most postmodernists, cannot invest depth or create truly satisfying artifacts if not also grounded in the mastery of craft so as to speak to levels beyond that small portion of mind, the conscious, and resonate with the unconscious and the body. Freud called dreams "the royal road to the unconscious," but it is through craft that the unconscious becomes a resource to be drawn on in creating compelling works and performances.

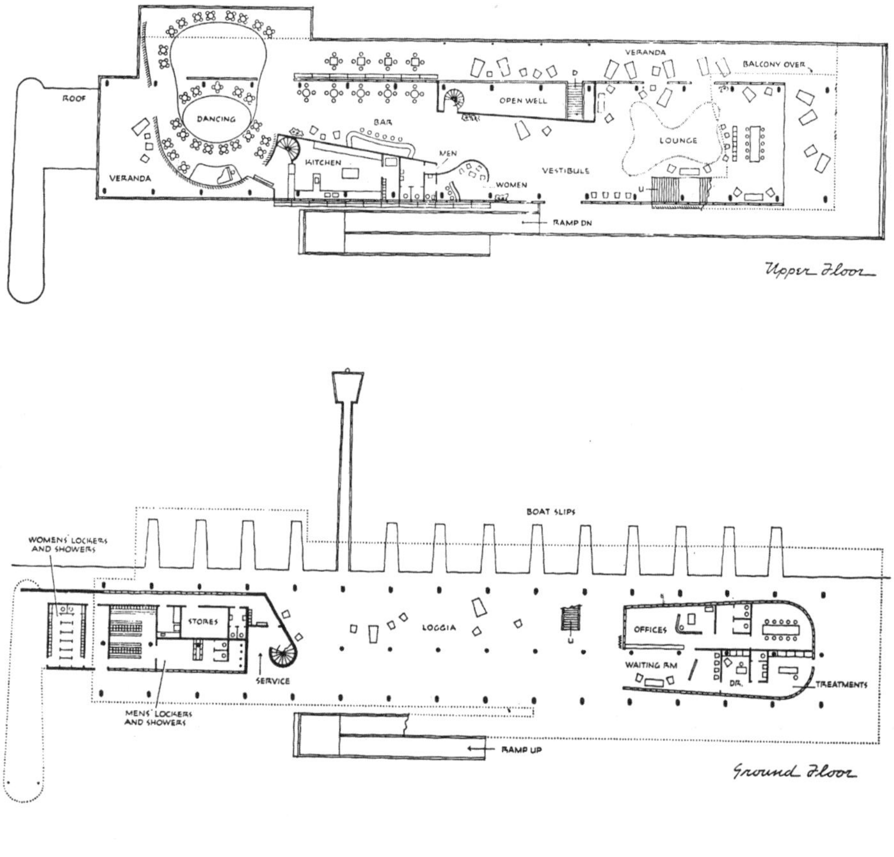

Plan for a yacht club, by Oscar Niemeyer, Rio de Janeiro

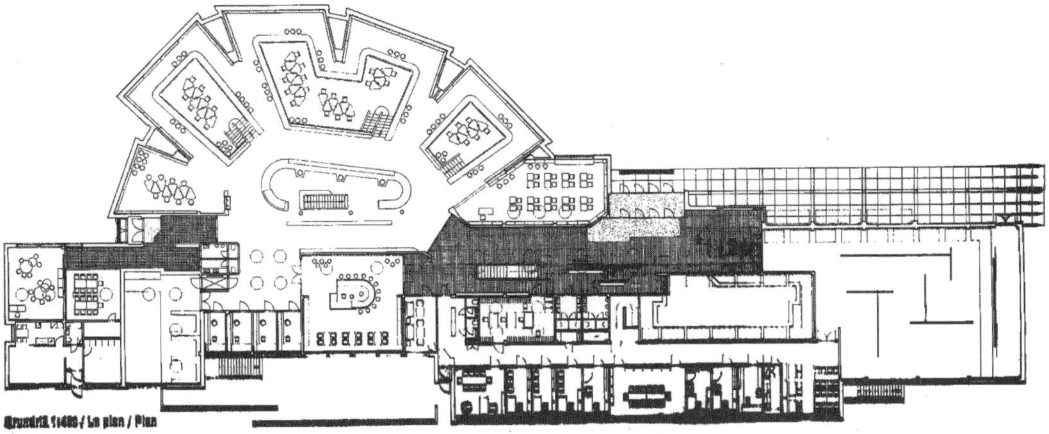

Plan for Rovaniemi Library, by Alvar Aalto, Rovaniemi, Finland

The quietly commanding presence of a well-crafted building, and the relationships that such buildings elicit with us, cannot be fully conveyed by illustrations in a book. Yet those who read drawings well can sense many of the qualities that result from well-crafted plans. Shaping these was once a skill central to modern architecture but is now a vanishing art, replaced by diagrammatic layouts or spurious shape-making. It thus seems apt to briefly discuss two beautifully crafted plans, one of an unbuilt project for a yacht club for Rio de Janeiro by Oscar Niemeyer and the other the Rovaniemi Library by Aalto. These contrast dramatically in character, partly in responding to very different programs and context. One is for hedonistic pursuits in the tropics and opens up to the views and the breezes that would waft through it; the other is a place of quiet study in a place of frigid winters and is introverted and softly lit from above. And although both plans are organized around pronounced processional routes on a diagonal bias, there are further contrasts.

With the yacht club, a predefined rectangular space below a sweeping roof is minimally articulated to host a range of activities in perfectly judged sequence and relationship to each other, and several of the articulating elements are curved to add dynamism to the flow of space and elicit a relationship with the people whom they guide and propel. Note particularly the choreographed flow from the open entry: you enter with the view over the bay ahead and down through a slot in the floor to the boat slips, are then greeted on the left by a forward-projecting curved wall, guided between people at the bar and those at tables overlooking the bay, and then presented with a flourish (ta-da!) into the middle of the restaurant/nightclub.

Aalto's library is almost the antithesis of Niemeyer's yacht club. Instead of loosely partitioning a given volume, the enclosing, embracing exterior form of the library is generated by the movement and activities within and the sculpting of the light from the large clerestories. From the wind lobby, where you immediately engage the building intimately in the act of shaking hands with its tactile door handles, you bear right across a clattery tile floor to be hushed as you step onto the library carpet. Like the control desk, the fan shape of the library distorts in recognition of the oblique entry. Indeed, the back wall seems pushed outward in response to your momentum and by the pressure of your gaze as you move into the room, much as a soap bubble distends with the direction of the breath, while the indents between the bays assert a countervailing pull inward to shorten the spans of the main beams.

If the curved elements of the yacht club propel the movement of space and people, the building also hangs back somewhat. By contrast, the engagement elicited by the library is much more intimate. This goes beyond leaning on the continuous countertops, including those that form reading desks capping the bookshelves around the sunken reading areas, and handling the books on the crammed shelves. As the forms of the building lead you through it, with tactile elements falling to hand just where you reach for them, it is almost as if you were breathing the building into form with your movement and gaze, your exhalations pushing the reading bays outward and your inhalations prompted by the constricting indents. The illusion of intimate participation in the formation of the building creates an extraordinary sense of identification with it.

If the yacht club represents an emancipatory functionalism, in which use is set free and only partially defined, the library represents a participatory functionalism, in which it seems that your very presence shapes it. These are just two of several approaches to serving function and evoking a relationship with the user found in mid-twentieth-century modern architecture, most of which are now largely forgotten. Both plans share an extraordinary, masterly precision, the product of accumulated prior experience by their architects as well as crafting through constant resketching. The result is a distilled and enriching synthesis that elicits relationships with the buildings at many levels, including those below the threshold of conscious awareness, even if you are consciously struck by the beauty and sense of inevitability both designs achieve.

Everything discussed above has profound implications for educating architects—including my introductory comments, the educational implications of which are beyond the scope of brief comment. Although ever more building materials are available, students have fewer opportunities to play with and experiment with them—to explore how to work them, how much they bend before creasing, how they feel in the hand or when the body leans against them, and so on—knowledge once intimately acquired of a small range of materials in the workshop and on the building site. Also, to move too soon from sketching on paper to the computer, or starting immediately on the computer, also robs the student or architect of the tactile and tentative groping and slow emergence of form, perhaps through a blur of smudged or overlaid lines, possible with soft pencil on paper.

Probably the biggest challenge to education is that all these dimensions of craft are best learned one to one, in an apprenticeship situation or an approximation of it in the academic studio. They cannot be taught in lectures or any multimedia format. This is particularly true of the craft of design, which you learn by sitting at the same desk and watching how someone who has mastered the craft thinks with his or her fingers, perhaps tracing patterns of movement and the pockets of activity they both connect and stir to life, then placing barriers where required and ensuring none where interaction between activities is preferred, and so on.

It is also only from the experienced that the student can learn about craft in the narrow sense in which many architects think of it, asking questions such as: What sizing and spacing of a component works best visually as well as structurally, and best harmonizes (or contrasts) with other such elements? How pronounced or played down should the junctions be? Should corners be rounded off or square, and if rounded, at what radius, and should the radius of the corners all be the same? No matter how talented a student is, he or she is bound to learn much from someone who has been pondering such judgments for years. And these are far from trivial points: they profoundly affect how a building feels and the quality of relationships it elicits.

But where to find such teachers, particularly when their skills are prized in practice, and how to find them in sufficient numbers now that schools and classes are so large? Also, in recent years schools have tended to hire academics who have pursued intellectual study on their way to doctorates rather than mastering the crafts of design and construction. In some schools this has led to a deep and unhealthy schism between the tenured academic staff and the part-time design tutors who are not around long enough for protracted personal engagement. The Ghost Lab workshops were an invaluable chance for deep immersion in learning how to handle tools and a limited range of materials, but they were not long enough to hone the craft skills that can be developed with such knowledge as a base. Yet the Ghost 13 works exemplify what can be achieved through the mastery of craft and so serve as inspiration to pursue such mastery.

To heal the ruptured world that is the legacy of modernity, much needs to be brought back into "right relationship." For architecture this means responding and becoming integral to place, even bringing the myriad forces that shape and act on it (from history to climate) into visible focus. Creating right relationship also requires mastery of craft, not just making things well, but giving due, yet not excessive emphasis, to each constructional component so that everything comes together in a deeply satisfying whole, one that rewards prolonged attention but does not insistently demand it. Bringing people back into right relationship with each other and the rest of the world means continuing to respect the individualism and privacy that modernity overemphasized, but also returning the many opportunities for harmonious and mutually beneficial interaction with other people and nature that modernity tended to suppress.

As Thomas Berry said, "The world is a communion of subjects, not a collection of objects."[2] Only by recognizing that will we come into right relationship with and be at home in the world, rather than alienated outsiders exploiting it.

1 See Juhani Pallasmaa, *The Thinking Hand* (West Sussex, UK: John Wiley & Sons, 2009), for a superb discussion of all this, especially the chapter "Embodied Thinking," which students would benefit from reading with deepening understanding at intervals through their studies.

2 Thomas Berry, "The Meadow Across the Creek," in *The Great Work: Our Way Into the Future* (New York: Bell Tower, 1999), 82.

Learning to Think

Ingerid Helsing Almaas

Ghost 13 participants listen to Ingerid Helsing Almaas's talk on pedagogy.

You can't fool the body.

The primary aim of the Ghost Architectural Laboratory has always been the education of architects. The digging and carrying, sawing and hammering, the thoughts, sketches, and discussions, the towers and barns, sheds and houses built at Shobac all have one main purpose: to provoke insight in students of architecture by engaging their bodies in the practice of building, and by turning their minds to the stories, facts, traditions, and challenges that might determine how we build.

Ghost 13: Ideas in Things seemed nothing less than an enacted manifesto, a conference played out in the same place and along the same lines as those previous laboratories. Surrounding the three days of presentations and discussions were tents, mud, dogs, wind, rain, and the close gravelly murmur of the Atlantic Ocean. Though we did not build, the invited practitioners who showed their work at Ghost 13 presented the results of thoughts and practices that over time seemed to circumscribe a common territory. Over the three days of gathering, this common ground became increasingly tangible—even more so because of the surroundings, the farm, the sheep, the cold barn, and the warm coffee; because of the grass and the timber, the music, and the dancing. And afterward we knew: we were there, together, and though the experience was limited to spoken words and pictures on a screen, something was made.

Representations

Traditionally, the subject of architecture is taught through representations, and the instruction of the skills regarded as necessary for practice happens as in a mirror: simulations of reality reflected in maps, drawings, and models. It is a game played with the tacit agreement of all parties—the teachers, the students, the surrounding profession—that the simulation is meaningful as a way to teach architecture. Only very rarely is this game disturbed. Most of the time the activities of an architecture school go on behind closed doors, with the occasional visitor from the outside world coming in to play their predefined part; a technical expert, a visiting architect, a guest critic.

In this conventional architectural training, a building is conceived of, developed, and presented as an image. Even with the most sophisticated 3-D technology, the building remains an imagined object, carefully composed and rendered, but nonetheless just a picture. It may well be that the production of such pictures is a necessary part of architectural training. After all, an architect needs to be able to imagine what the world will be like, and present those imaginings to other people. But if the full extent of an architect's training is conducted in this way, through representations of mental edifices unchallenged by the messy and conflicting demands of reality, only luck will decide whether that architect is able to make any significant contribution to the real world.

Because obviously, even the smallest piece of built architecture is shaped by a whole host of surrounding forces: material, financial, social, political, emotional, etc., and architecture students need to be introduced to these forces and learn to deal with them in order to make a positive contribution to the world in which we live. And to quote Juhani Pallasmaa's Ghost 13 keynote address: "The essential task of architecture is to improve the world that we live in, to make it a better place for ourselves."[1]

These many forces that shape architecture are not easily represented. The increasing use of diagrams and flowcharts in student projects may signal an increased awareness that there is more going on in any given situation than can be conveyed in a conventional site plan. But though many of these mappings may be insightful, they do not necessarily teach students much about what happens when they actually have to engage in a situation as active agents.

For that experience, they need to be out there. They need to be given the time, the trust, and the guidance to take part in reality, be allowed to change it, and to feel the responsibility that comes with changing the way people live and do things.

Education

It is through *doing* that you test your presumptions and the consequences of your actions, in architectural education as in all other areas of life.

This is where construction, like the Ghost laboratories, endeavors, not only offering valuable lessons: it is *essential* for an architect to grapple with the physical world. The experience offered by physical building practice is indispensable in architectural education. And, as Juhani Pallasmaa pointed out: the craft of building is not just a case of the thought guiding the hand, as the architect's thought by extension guides the craftsman's hand, it is also a case of *the hand guiding the thought*. As you work, you think. And if you don't work, if you don't move your own hands and feel the weight of lumber and concrete with your own body, you won't understand what architecture is.

Obviously, the aim of making architects build is not to make them craftsmen, in the same way that teaching them philosophy is not to make them philosophers and teaching them statics is not to make them engineers. Architecture is a synthetic discipline, messy, "impure," as Pallasmaa often states, "because it contains inherently irreconcilable ingredients, such as metaphysical, cultural, and economic aspirations, functional, technical, and aesthetic objectives."[2] The task of architecture is to bring these ingredients *together* and, through a physical construction, make life better. And for that, architects need to understand as many aspects of the synthesis as possible, from the philosophical to the physical.

A Space for Questions

Most architects will eventually develop some idea of this, in time, once they get out of school. But, paradoxically, there is a real advantage to engaging in physical construction while still in school, even though it can never be "real." School offers the luxury of selective conditions. Education is not, and should not be, a simulation of practice. Yes, architecture school is the ground for the transfer of professional knowledge, but it is also a space where there are no limits to the questions asked. And if we accept that architects are charged with improving life, rather than simply confirming the status quo, then intelligent questions become as important as encyclopedic knowledge. How can you improve if you do not question?

Learning architecture through physical construction does not limit the necessity for questioning, for challenging what we see, think, and do. You do not stop thinking when you pick up a hammer. In fact, you could argue that it is precisely because architects are not professional craftsmen that they have so much to learn by building. Had they been better builders, they would learn less. Had they known the techniques and processes, had their operations with tools and materials been automated, professionalized, there would be no room for thoughts to drift in, no need to exchange words, to discuss and reflect. One of the strengths of the Ghost laboratories is precisely that most of the participants are amateurs, and so, thankfully, they are slow. As you step back from the wall and let the hammer sink for a moment, wondering what to do next, there is time for questions.

Even the structures of the Ghost labs can be thought of as questions. Why build a tower by the shore? Why build it on a hill? Why move a barn, why leave an old stone wall where it is, why cast a plinth, raise a wall? Because the consequences of building actions are physical and endure in time, the questions need to be good. And the answers even better. Once something is built, you will know, immediately, whether the questions were relevant, and whether the answers were good enough. You can't fool the body.

The Ghost laboratories represent a strong position, a clear critique, and a productive counter-proposition to the priorities dominating mainstream architectural education. Stones have been laid. The many participants in the enacted manifesto of Ghost 13, the conversations carried out both from the podium and in the audience, people both speaking and listening, have mapped out a possible curriculum for another way of thinking, another way of doing architecture.

1 Juhani Pallasmaa, "Architecture and the Human Nature—searching for a sustainable metaphor," keynote address, Ghost 13 conference, Nova Scotia, June 14–17, 2011.

2 Ibid.

The Value of Beauty in Architecture

Christine Macy

The Barn was lit up for Ghost 13 night sessions.

Certainly, the siting of Ghost 13 was unforgettable—a foggy coastal landscape of windswept bluffs, roaring surf, and grazing sheep. And the community in the rustic circular barn felt warm and welcoming—over two hundred students, practitioners, and aficionados of architecture assembled to hear exceptional architects from across North America, Australia, and West Africa speak about their work. The enthusiasm and passion in the wind- and rain-battered barn was palpable. Who couldn't help but feel this was an extraordinary gathering of people and ideas? Yet it was the images that were the focus of the event. Projected into the darkened space, slide after slide brought us to sites and places around the world, to witness and experience works of architecture through the eyes of their creators.

The pictures were beautiful. Well lit, well framed, well photographed, they showed houses made of simple or sumptuous materials in spectacular settings. The works of architecture transformed landscapes into sweeping panoramas or, just as effortlessly, focused attention on fragile ground covers or exposed rock outcroppings. The architecture modulated our imagined movements through these homes, making them (and us) feel measured and poetic. It arrested our gaze and transfixed our attention, focusing our awareness on texture, light, color, and material.

In reflecting on the Ghost 13 conference—and the works these exceptional architects shared with each other—I came to realize that a big part of this event was about beauty, created through the craft of well-designed houses. Ghost 13 spoke to the value of beauty in architecture.

The Purpose of Architecture

When architecture critics write about beauty, they often turn to the evocation of experience—as I did in the first paragraphs of this essay. Yet the concept of beauty as a feeling is only one view of the matter, albeit one with a long tradition in the West. Back in the 1930s, Ananda Coomaraswamy, who was at that time a curator at the Boston Museum of Fine Arts, wrote about a theory of art that he saw as being fundamental to all cultures since the beginning of human artistic activity. Setting aside religious art (which is a large portion of traditional artistic production), he investigated the art of everyday objects, such as a bowl, a weapon, an item of clothing, or a dwelling. Although such items are made to be used, they are also, according to Coomaraswamy, "philosophically linked to the inner life of a people" through their form or ornamentation.[1] In most cultures in the world, objects are considered well made when they successfully express a concept or idea. In this worldview, art is thought of as "rhetoric," or a kind of knowledge. In the West however, we call it *aesthetic* and think of art as a kind of feeling.[2] The Greek word "aesthetic," Coomaraswamy says, refers to a perception by the senses, especially by feeling. To identify our approach to art with feelings is to apply art only to the life of pleasure and to disconnect it from the active and contemplative lives.[3] Rhetoric, on the other hand, implies that "what is said or made must be effective, and must work, or would not have been worth saying or making."[4]

So when we in the West think of art as an aesthetic experience, rather than as a well made idea, we create a false opposition between beauty and utility. We separate art from its place at the center of culture, where everyone understands that it serves its purpose well, and we put it in a marginal position where beauty is in the eye of the beholder. In the history of humankind, a beautiful object has been something that is correctly and well-made, which expresses an idea and serves its purpose well.[5] And in architectural history, well-designed buildings have always been repositories of meaning. And the title of the Ghost 13 conference—"Ideas in Things"—recognized this.

The Craft of Architecture

Craft is required for something to be correctly and well made. Coomaraswamy again:

> The word *ingenium*, translated by "innate skill"...is the source of our word "engineer," and... the medieval concept of artistry is, in fact, far more like our conception of engineering than it is like our [present-day] concept of "art": the traditional artificer's business is to make things that will work, and not merely please, whether the body or the mind. He was, in fact, a builder of bridges for both at once, and these bridges were expected to bear the weights for which they were designed; their beauty depended upon their perfection as works of art, not their perfection on their beauty.[6]

Craft, of course, is not simply a matter of repeating a known formula. Each work of architecture has its causes, which include the requirement of the commission, the architectural idea, and the materials and the means employed. Just as each commission is unique, so too is each site, the materials employed, and, of course, the architectural idea that directs the creation of the work. In this, each designer has an opportunity to demonstrate his or her skill.

> Invention, or intuition, is the discovery...of particular applications of first principles, all of which applications are implicitly contained in those principles, only awaiting the occasion [to be revealed]....Every commission demands a corresponding invention. But this invention is not more the artificer's "own" than is the occasion that demanded it; it is a discovery of *the* right way of solving a given problem, and not a private way.[7]

Private houses for well-to-do clients who are passionate about architecture have long provided an opportunity for architects to perfect their artistry in the design and detailing of space, materials, and assemblies. Shim-Sutcliffe's Integral House in Toronto is an excellent example of the level of artistry achievable under favorable circumstances. In this work, they were given the opportunity to pursue the relationship between digital and handcraft in a house that explored the resonance between music and architecture. On a tighter budget, Olson Kundig conceived of the Chicken Point Cabin in northern Idaho as an "instrument" to be played through mechanical devices configured into the building—sharing, as Tom Fisher points out in his contribution to this volume, that the perfection of architectural craftsmanship can be equally found in dwellings made with modest means.[8] In both cases, as Peter Buchanan reminds us, craft is skill that is matured through patient repetition and practice.[9]

The Appreciation of Architecture

The final aspect of art that Coomaraswamy considers is its appreciation. Of the two sorts of pleasure—what we experience through our senses and what we understand in a work—it is the latter we have in mind when we think of culture. The pleasure of comprehension does not infringe on...the pleasure of the senses, but includes a very great deal more than that.... Once we understand a work of art from all these points of view we can derive intellectual pleasure from the sight of something that has been "well and truly made."[10]

The projects shown at Ghost 13: Ideas in Things were exceptional for the way they elicited both kinds of pleasure: sensory delight in color, composition, material, framing human activities and sites, and the intellectual pleasure of seeing architectural ideas realized with exceptional craft and artistry. The conference, and this publication, is an opportunity to reflect on the ideas that inform well-made things, and to critically engage in a discussion of the purpose and craft that goes into the making of a timeless architecture.

1 Ananda Coomaraswamy, "A Figure of Speech or a Figure of Thought?" in *Coomaraswamy, Vol. 1, Traditional Art and Symbolism, Selected Papers*, ed. Roger Lipsey (Princeton, NJ: Princeton University Press Bollingen Series, 1977), 13.

2 Ibid.

3 Ibid.

4 Ibid., 14.

5 Ibid., 27.

6 Coomaraswamy, "The Philosophy of Medieval and Oriental Art," in *Coomaraswamy, Vol. 1*, ed. Lipsey, 49.

7 Ibid., 49–50.

8 Thomas Fisher, "Seeing the World Whole," in this volume, 13–20.

9 Peter Buchanan, "Construction and Composition, Concept versus Craft," in this volume, 185–93.

10 Coomaraswamy, "The Philosophy of Medieval and Oriental Art," 62–63.

The Urgency of Ghost 13: Ideas in Things

Essy Baniassad

Children attending the first type of school space, an open-air school, in Benares, India.

Every institution of any form and content, social or intellectual, tends to ossify in time, to drift away from its primary purpose, and to become an impediment to any other primal purpose and vision. It takes a conscious process of continuous deconstruction and resynthesis to resist the drift, and a bold total break with the institution to reverse it.[1] CIAM and Ghost 13, among other subsequent events, are, in various degrees, instances of such a process.

The process of this drift is subtle and indistinct since it is an accumulated result of many steps, each one of which in itself may be progressive and well intentioned. But the effect of it, whether in the area of ideas, designs, or education, is evident in the fading glow at the origin of things. Architectural education has been particularly affected by such a drift, due to the increasing replacement of direct observation of reality, the *thing*, with its abstract familiar derivative, the *idea*. One correlated effect has been the displacement of learning through exploration by one based on received information, and the changes of schools from centers of discourse and discovery to "academic" corporations. In this process, the proverbial school gathering under a tree—the one-room schoolhouse—has become a labyrinth, the main challenge of which, once you're in it, seems to be to find your way out: "on the road," under the sky, under the tree again. There the aim of education is to inspire not to impress, to reveal not to obscure, to extend not to confine, to celebrate not to judge.

The Summer Arts Institute faculty of Black Mountain College gathers in North Carolina in 1946. From left to right: Leo Amino, Jacob Lawrence, Leo Lionni, Ted Dreier, Nora Lionni, Beaumont Newhall, Gwendolyn Lawrence, Ise Gropius, Jean Varda (in tree), Nancy Newhall (sitting), Walter Gropius, Mary "Molly" Gregory, Josef Albers, and Anni Albers.

By contrast the new institutional environment tends to replace knowledge and the reality of things with codes, names, labels, conventions, and rhetorical illusions.

Restoring reality to such illusion has been the motive behind the modernist impulse throughout history. This is not associated with modernism as a style, but rather the timeless impulse to remove the haze of history, the established norms and notions, and to regain the childlike physical directness, the "gemlike flame" of untamed imagination.[2] Thus modernism reaches for the primal origins and the existential necessity of primitive originality.[3]

In both form and content the modernist movements and events assume a conscious distance from conventional settings, formats, and orthodoxies, to guard against drifting into the very conventions that they intend to question. This is key to understanding the nature of such movements and their relationship with established institutions. CIAM, Black Mountain College, Ghost Lab, and other such initiatives are not retreats as their settings might suggest. They are staging points with the vision to see, question, engage, influence, and arrest the drift away from the primary purpose of architecture and education, while standing outside of it.[4]

Ghost 13, "Ideas in Things," challenged post-CIAM positions in current architectural practice, education, and educational institutions, including many that, while rooted in modernism, have been gradually institutionalized. It did so through a diverse selection of fresh and pioneering work by practicing architects and presentations on architectural history, theory, and criticism.

The presentations and proceedings were not particularly seeking to define a singular position and point of view. What was important here was not agreement or disagreement, but the intensity and sincerity of the proceedings. In a world defined by adopted metaphors of public relations and conventions of corporate and consumer culture, such sincerity and seriousness is itself a radical offering.[5] It is the necessary condition to reach past niceties and conventions of ideas and events, and to see the naked idea in the object. The aim of "Ideas in Things" was not the reaffirmation of what is known. It was the discovering of what is obscured by what is known, what is denied by what is offered, and what is excluded by what has become commonplace practice.

Ghost 13 raised a fundamental question that concerns the understanding and engagement with the modernist impulse in any form. How was it that modernism, the impulse to question conventionality, was itself smoothed and vulgarized into a convention, orthodoxy, and an institution? Surely not simply because of the actions of a small group of "pioneers." It engaged innumerable individual designers, many with a spirit of curiosity, originality, choice, rejection, and critical selection. But there were obviously many more who trained on the deep-seated tendency to see things only in the form of orthodoxies or styles, and they tended to search for a convenient convention to adopt, a form to follow. It was ultimately this tendency that subverted the point of modernism, and formed a new one in the course of its opposition to an existing institution and style.

That training was founded on a style-based view of history, which could only register change in terms of a style; it not only obscured a true sense of history, but it delegitimized it as a foundation of architectural knowledge. The rich ordered chaos of reality lies beyond one view's reach and range. What it offers is a memoriam to the things past, rather than the eternal presence and relevance of all that exists, date of origin and passage of time notwithstanding; to quote Wallace Stevens, "all history is modern history."[6]

This is where education comes in, and the urgency of the theme of "Ideas in Things" comes into focus. It reaffirmed the primal purpose of architecture, where the need for shelter and commodity is ennobled with human aspirations of immortality. It implicitly pointed out the urgency of architecture and its demise where it has been codified, commodified, and institutionalized.

The theme of "Ideas in Things" questions the content of school programs, in their realism and abstractions, as they engage in imaginary worlds and turn away from imaginative observation of discovery and design in the real world. Virginia Woolf's comment on the relation between the two worlds comes to mind: "We may enjoy our room in the tower, with the painted walls and the commodious bookcases, but down in the garden there is a man digging who buried his father this morning, and it is he and his like who live the real life and speak the real language."[7]

The presentations on design, history and theory, and technology were directed at the status quo in education. They were not statements meant to affirm a further orthodoxy nor to propose a manifesto, but to open the window, as Van Eyck would say. Above all, the most sharply posed question was one implied in the title: "Ideas in Things." It recalls the well-known distinction between the Cartesian versus the Existentialist position: "I think therefore I am" versus "I am therefore I think." It also invites a close interrogation of the relationship between languages and physical forms; that is, works of architecture as distinct from literature or science.

In architecture many iconic statements are slogans, metaphors, or riddles whose meaning depends on a key that lies outside the statement and the commonly understood meaning of the words. Such statements are more in the genre of poetry than prose. Some thing, a real entity independent of words, is the key to the riddle. Some of these well-known statements are: "less is more," "form follows function," "house is a machine for living," and "decoration is crime," etc. The key to the understanding of the phrase "house is a machine for living" is in the design of some actual houses, rather than in the narrow meaning of the word "machine." Therefore the meaning changes in each case depending on the designer and the actual design. It hardly extends architectural understanding of the work of Le Corbusier. To base an extensive argument on the ordinary meaning of the word "machine" or on "less is more" in a literary sense shows a misunderstanding at best. In all such cases the "idea" is not independent of the real "thing."[8]

In architecture, the language of words is a supporting language, but a necessary one for intelligent discourse about "the thing," design and form, as in the design studio. And that makes the dual "idea-thing" a key concept in the formulation of any program. Despite its appearance this juxtaposition does not pose an irresolvable polarity. "Idea" and "thing" together are elements of a more complex idea-thing concept, the understanding of which is key to safeguarding the studio against realism, a pitfall to which the studio is often susceptible in the attempt to deal with reality. The distinction is well expressed in the words of Wallace Stevens, that "Realism is a corruption of reality."[9]

The work and the workings of the studios of the architects who participated in Ghost Lab illustrated the difference and provided examples for valuable reference. Glenn Murcutt's practice is a clear example of a "studio" at work. His explicit comments should be seen in the context of the passion and the precision that glows in every instance of his work. Similarly the designs by a host of other participating architects offer potent examples, which address the deeper reality of primal conditions in architecture, not disregarding the necessity of transient functions. These are not so much architectural commissions as they are experiments in architectural design, much like explorations in the scientific study of natural phenomena. They go beyond contingent questions and deal with them within a context of essential ones. For them economy is an aesthetic issue not a question of monetary value, and function is defined in cultural norms not anecdotal requirements. Social conditions and imperatives are seen and addressed through their evidence in built form not in received statistics and theories.

For these reasons the study of architecture is ultimately the study of works of architecture and the history of architecture is composed of the body of all such work.

Significantly, the examples of the work presented are all designs for "the house." The house, as the built form of "dwelling," is the seminal form in architecture, in that every building is an extension of it. It is a collection of three primal places of human habitat: place of gathering, place of work, and place of solitude. All three places could be in one space, or one place could dominate depending on the primary function of the "house," assembly, theater, etc. Every value and mythology behind the house extends to every building, and no building, as an extension of the house, becomes a mere diagram of a function; the house is less anecdotal than an expression of a holistic vision of architecture. That vision originates not in "Adam's House in Paradise," but in the human primitive home on earth.[10] There lies the founding myths of human civilization and the seeds of culture. And the way to study them is to track their embodiment in the total scope of architecture—the house and the city—in their profound material reality; neither to receive them as theoretical abstractions nor to regard them as marketable commodities, but in the history of the subject—Architecture—that defines them and is defined by them. Architectural history is the home of the social, cultural, and ethical content of architecture and its embodiment in each individual work. It is one that embraces life in all its chaos and diversity and brings the past to life as a part of the present. It evolves out of the eternal presence of the origin of the human habitat and underlies all phases of its development in all scales.

As Juhani Pallasmaa notes, "architecture withers when it departs too far from the primary experiences and images of dwelling."[11] It may appear that my stress on the design studio might marginalize the relevance of other subjects in a program. The increasing abundance of information offers rich material for reference and learning. In architecture there is little to teach and much to learn. The increasing number of courses is a further aspect of the institutional drift. It dismembers the subject and reduces the intellectual challenge and the opportunity for exploration. The primary question for a program is how many divisions offer a useful path to study the scope, the complexity, and the unity of the subject. The three-part curriculum—place, craft, community—as suggested by Brian MacKay-Lyons is a good beginning. It identifies the essential domains in a program and guards against teaching too much, recognizing mathematician Alfred Whitehead's advice: "Do not teach too many subjects," and again, "What you teach, teach thoroughly."[12]

The clutter of courses and extensive "teaching," however well intentioned, often tends to reduce the courses to mere dissemination of information. It disturbs the solitude the student needs to assimilate and reconstruct the subject. It defeats its own educational objective as it interrupts the natural process of learning, a process with its own inner rhythm. It often brings back to me this childhood memory:

In Iran many relatives who came to visit us would take away cuttings of some quite special roses in our garden to plant in theirs. During a lunch visit my brother asked someone who had taken cuttings a couple of months earlier how the roses were doing. "Not well" she said, "they haven't even begun to grow roots." I wondered how she knew that. I asked, "How do you know they haven't begun to take root?" She said, "I take them out every week and check them."

1 "In the history of education, the most striking phenomenon is that schools of learning, which at one epoch are alive with a ferment of genius, in a succeeding generation exhibit merely pedantry and routine." Alfred North Whitehead, *The Aims of Education and Other Essays* (New York: Simon and Schuster, 1967).

2 Walter Pater. "To burn always with this hard gemlike flame, to maintain this ecstasy, is success in life."

3 This should not be mistaken for being stuck in the past. It echoes the modernist impulse to connect back to the primal origins of art. I regard "primitive" as a primal and pre-history or without-history quality inherent in a work and not related to its date. The modernist strives to be free from history and draws upon the primitive for inspiration. The place of "the primitive" is little considered in the formal history of architecture. It is however a key notion in Wilhelm Worringer's *Abstraction and Empathy*. "Primitive man"—which Worringer did not mean condescendingly—stands "lost and spiritually helpless amidst the things of the external world." But from this helplessness he draws the vitality to create the "greatest abstract beauty." Objects are removed from their natural context "with elementary necessity and in an individual form turned into art." See Sebastian Preuss, "Spiritual Intoxication," *ArtMag* 56 (August 2009), an essay on Wilhelm Worringer and Modernism. An example and influence of primitive origins in art is of course Picasso's work. The false view of "origins" as inconsequential and of negligible cultural impact is the key to the banality and failure of any work adhering to it. By contrast the reconnection to the primal origin in art continues to be a source of energy and vitality as exemplified in the work of Jean-Michel Basquiat.

4 The Black Mountain College initiative by John Andrew Rice was another notable example. Established in 1933 in North Carolina, Black Mountain College operated until 1957. It had an experimental program combining academic knowledge and practical skills. Josef and Anni Albers, Walter Gropius (Bauhaus), John Cage, and Buckminster Fuller taught there. The board included Albert Einstein and William Carlos Williams. From 1954 to 1957, Charles Olson and Robert Creeley published a literary journal, *Black Mountain Review*, with contributions by Allen Ginsberg, Jack Kerouac, William Burroughs, Gary Snyder, et al.

5 Recollection of the point by Susan Sontag in "Simone Weil," *The New York Review of Books* (February 1963).

6 Wallace Stevens, *Opus Posthumous: Poems, Plays, Prose*, ed. Samuel French Morse (New York: Alfred A. Knopf, 1957).

7 Virginia Woolf, "Montaigne," in *The Common Reader* (London: Hogarth Press, 1925).

8 This point underlies Ludwig Wittgenstein's statement, in *Tractatus Logico-Philosophicus* (London: Routledge, 1922): "What can be shown cannot be said," and in Daniel Barenboim's essay "Beethoven and the Quality of Courage": "It must be understood that one cannot explain the nature or the message of music through words"; Daniel Barenboim, *The New York Review of Books* (April 4, 2013).

9 To paraphrase Northrup Frye's understanding of Wallace Stevens, "Realism should be distinguished from Reality: Realism is a surrender of imagination to the external world; Imaginary world: imagination running away from the reality; 'The purely realistic mind never experiences any passion for reality.'" See Northrop Frye, *Spiritus Mundi: Essays on Literature, Myth, and Society* (Indianapolis: Indiana University Press, 1983), 278.

10 "In 1753, Marc Antoine Laugier, the French theorist, proposed the primitive hut as the foundation of architecture in his Essai sur l'architecture. See Joseph Rykwert, *On Adam's House in Paradise: The Idea of the Primitive Hut in Architectural History* (Greenwich, CT: New York Graphic Society and Museum of Modern Art, 1972).

11 Juhani Pallasmaa, "Architecture and Human Nature: A Call for a Sustainable Metaphor," in this volume, 31–40.

12 Whitehead, *The Aims of Education*.

Afterword: The Artist, the Artisan, and the Activist

Brian MacKay-Lyons and Robert McCarter

In the architectural press before and after Ghost 13 there were high expectations for this gathering of nearly two hundred distinguished architectural practitioners, professors, students, engineers, builders, clients, landscape architects, members of the press, and others. The density of great work from twenty-six diverse peers from around the world actually limited the time for debate. Judging from the response of the many colleagues in attendance, it was a magical experience (despite the cold, wet weather).

But what did we accomplish? Did the event live up to Cathleen McGuigan's challenge in *Architectural Record*: "Plotting a New Course for Architecture"? Did a unified position or manifesto emerge? Were there implications for architectural education? Is it even reasonable, in these seemingly relativistic times, to expect to resolve the problems of our discipline after a presentation-packed few days?

At the event, there was a great deal of agreement about architectural core values and disciplinary principles. (Some will call it preaching to the choir.) The theme of "ideas in things" united us like a call to battle. We believe that our discipline has come undone, that an unwholesome gulf has opened between the academy and practice in architecture. And we share a deep and passionate belief that our discipline should not be disembodied or dismembered. Throughout the sessions, speakers repeatedly referred to our disciplinary duty to learn from those who have gone before us in the practice of architecture—"paying respect to our elders," Peter Stutchbury called it. We noted how fundamentally important it is that the professional and academic discipline of architecture regain its ethical footing, and the presentations provided numerous examples of how ethics are deeply embedded in every decision regarding place, craft, and community—thereby embodying Ludwig Wittgenstein's assertion that "aesthetics and ethics are one and the same."[1]

There was also a great deal of agreement about what constitutes comprehensive, formal, professional design skill and what constitutes meaningful beauty—this at a time when our discipline seems to favor a technocratic, unsynthesized fracturing of architecture into its isolated aspects (sustainability, social program, digital representation, formal fashion, and so on). Insistence on the unity of the field was evident in the Ghost 13 themes: place, craft, and community. Each speaker—whether architect or critic—was reasonably comfortable speaking to the particular theme that his or her work is often associated with, while recognizing that all architecture of quality is an artful synthesis of all of these thematic aspects. The architect must be simultaneously the artist, the artisan, and the activist.

In addition to our common belief in the *unity* of place, craft, and community, the Ghost 13 participants expressed a general acceptance of the *comprehensiveness* of these themes—a belief that, at a high level, these robust "content buckets" map over the discipline of architecture as a whole.

We understand *place* as landscape (natural and cultural), light, climate response, geomorphology, flora, fauna, and environmental sustainability. The environment is not merely the setting for human inhabitation; rather, the environment and the inhabitant are unified and synthesized in the making and experience of place. Place is involved in the creation of atmosphere, ambiance, mood, and memory, as well as the cultivation and preservation of spaces of inhabitation, thereby forming the basis for our individual and collective identity. Architecture may be defined as the humanistic art of *place-making*, a constructive act that allows each of us to dwell in the world in a way that is truly sustainable in the full sense of the word. This connectedness to place is an essential source of authentic content—something that is now even more critical in the face of the superficial placelessness associated with global civilization.

We understand *craft* as a connection to the master builder tradition, where the art of architecture is inseparable from the embodied experience, the thinking hand, tactility, sensuality, the social act of building, material culture, building well, the building industry as the medium of architecture, and ecological sustainability. "Craft is the resolution of natural, cultural, and economic demands and opportunities," as Tom Kundig said; this involves fit, finish, and proportion—things learned "by hand" as part of what we might call "crafting the experience." As a part of place-making, craft often involves the reengagement of existing craft and material traditions so as to allow new uses. The quality of craft and construction is understood to directly affect the experience of the inhabitant, through the intimacy of detail and the marks of human craftsmanship. For the architect, the builder, and the occupants, "building is a form of knowing," as Patricia Patkau noted. Craft is more ethical than technical in nature, involving an understanding of economy that makes the most of the resources at hand, the reuse of what we already have, and an engagement of Frank Lloyd Wright's insight that "limitations are the architect's best friend."[2] A result of this broadened and deepened definition of craft is the paradoxical combination of "tranquility and vitality" that Kenneth Frampton finds in Wright's work.

We understand *community* as it is expressed through participatory design, social agency, urbanism, design/build experience, and ritual architecture as a sustainable art. A community has its roots in all the dwellings of all those who have inhabited this place before us, and the sustainability of a community depends on learning the lessons their dwellings can teach us. Every community is in some ways unique, having developed as an appropriate response to its particular material culture, environmental context, and the character of its members—a fact that is too often overlooked in the increasing homogenization of our contemporary globalized condition. Building sustainable communities involves understanding the critical difference between what we *can* do and what we *should* do. The community, as the group that commissions public buildings, is critical to the existence and continuity of any culture of architecture. Building community also requires architecture to communicate with everyone. Building community involves making an architecture that fits itself into the situation at hand, modestly building on what was there before, but that also results in the world being made a better place through each constructive act.

While the theme of "ideas in things" applies across the discipline of architecture, the artificial separation of theory and practice—thinking and making—in universities today has led to schools of architecture where no *thing* is made. The super-realistic digital representations typical in schools today "deaden imagination," as Patricia Patkau has pointed out, and keep the students at an insurmountable distance from the act of making that is so essential to architecture. Those who teach architecture in many universities today "could not build a bookcase with their own hands," as the late Raimund Abraham put it.[3] We should remember that architecture has been an apprenticeship-based discipline for far longer than it has been a university-trained profession; this ancient but vibrant master builder–based "tradition of practice" characterizes the work of the best contemporary architects. Architectural education remains a fraught issue. The Ghost design/build workshops were founded as a response to the lack of making in universities.

The comprehensiveness of the themes of place, craft, and community recommends itself as an answer to Rick Joy's question, "What is the curriculum for architectural education now?" To those who would argue that architectural education was not dealt with directly at Ghost 13, we say that the whole conference was about education, through a bold articulation of what an enacted and built curriculum for architecture looks like, now and always. In fact, St. John's Church, the octagonal troop barn, and the restaurants and bars of Lunenburg functioned as our one-room schoolhouses.

We experienced the Ghost sessions during the event itself, and in this book, less as a manifesto than as a performance felt through all of the senses. Like a multiday theatrical or musical performance, the conference participants played out the curriculum and enacted the disciplinary principles, ritually reconfirming our common architectural values, before departing to carry on the good fight as artists, artisans, and activists in our schools, practices, and communities. It was like "The Last Waltz," the concert at the Winterland Ballroom in San Francisco in 1976, when The Band and a varied group of respected friends gathered to celebrate their craft. There is no Ghost sessions manifesto, only the music.

1 Ludwig Wittgenstein, *Tractatus Logico-Philosophicus* (London: Routledge, 1922), 183.
2 Frank Lloyd Wright, *The Future of Architecture* (New York: Horizon, 1953), 62.
3 Raimund Abraham, interview with Kenneth Frampton, *Newsline: Columbia University Graduate School of Architecture, Planning, and Preservation* (January 1990).

Contributors

Ingerid Helsing Almaas is an architect and the editor of *Arkitektur N*, the Norwegian Review of Architecture.

Steve Badanes is cofounder of Jersey Devil Design/Build and holds the Howard S. Wright Endowed Chair at University of Washington, where he directs the Neighborhood Design/Build studio.

Essy Baniassad is professor emeritus at Dalhousie University School of Architecture and Planning and research professor in the department of architecture at the Chinese University of Hong Kong.

Deborah Berke is the founding partner at Deborah Berke Partners and an adjunct professor of architectural design at Yale University.

Marlon Blackwell is principal at Marlon Blackwell Architect and serves as distinguished professor and department head at the University of Arkansas School of Architecture.

Peter Buchanan is an author, historian, and critic, who has worked as an architect and urban designer-planner in various parts of Africa, Europe, and the Middle East for a decade, and was an editor and writer at the *Architectural Press* and deputy editor at *Architectural Review*.

Wendell Burnette is principal at Wendell Burnette Architects and professor of practice at the design school at Arizona State University.

Thomas Fisher is professor and dean of the college of design at the University of Minnesota.

Ted Flato is cofounder and partner at Lake | Flato Architects.

Kenneth Frampton is the Ware Professor of Architecture at Columbia University's Graduate School of Architecture, Planning, and Preservation, and author of several books on architectural criticism.

Andrew Freear is the Wiatt Professor at Auburn University and director of the Rural Studio since 2002.

Ghost Architectural Laboratory was an international architectural education center in Kingsburg, Nova Scotia, and was in operation from 1994 to 2011.

Vincent James is a principal at VJAA and the Cass Gilbert Professor-in-Practice at the University of Minnesota School of Architecture.

Rick Joy is principal at Rick Joy Architect.

Francis Kéré is principal at Kéré Architecture and lectures at Technische Universität Berlin.

Richard Kroeker is principal at Richard Kroeker Design and professor of practice at Dalhousie University School of Architecture and Planning.

Tom Kundig is a founding partner of Olson Kundig Architects.

Brian MacKay-Lyons is the founding partner at MacKay-Lyons Sweetapple Architects and a professor at Dalhousie University School of Architecture and Planning.

Christine Macy is dean of the Dalhousie University School of Architecture and Planning.

Robert McCarter is a practicing architect and author, and the Ruth and Norman Moore Professor of Architecture at Washington University in St. Louis.

David Miller is a founding partner of The Miller Hull Partnership and the professor and chair of the department of architecture at the University of Washington.

Glenn Murcutt was awarded the twenty-sixth annual Pritzker Prize in 2002 and is professor of practice at the University of New South Wales in Australia.

Juhani Pallasmaa is principal at Arkkitehtitoimisto Juhani Pallasmaa, has taught at universities around the world, and is the author of many books on architecture and phenomenology.

Patricia Patkau is cofounder of Patkau Architects and emeritus professor at the school of architecture and landscape architecture at University of British Columbia.

Dan Rockhill is executive director of Studio 804 and the J. L. Constant Distinguished Professor of Architecture at the University of Kansas.

Brigitte Shim is cofounder and principal of Shim-Sutcliffe Architects and an associate professor at the University of Toronto's John H. Daniels Faculty of Architecture, Landscape, and Design.

Peter Stutchbury is principal at Peter Stutchbury Architecture and is conjoint professor in architecture at the University of Newcastle.

Jennifer Yoos is a principal at VJAA and professor-in-practice at the University of Minnesota School of Architecture.

Acknowledgments

Teamwork: Ghost 13 speakers gather to help a colleague pull her car out of a pond.

This book and the conference that it documents have been a labor of love for me over the past few years—love for architecture and love for the community of colleagues and friends who have made them possible. One morning over breakfast in 2009, when Glenn Murcutt received the AIA Gold Medal in Washington, D.C., I asked him if the unconditional generosity among the architects whose work is featured here is typical in the history of our discipline. He answered that, in his view, it was and is unique.

First among these colleagues is my partner Talbot Sweetapple, who acted as master of ceremonies at the conference and who supports these distractions from the business of our practice. Thanks to historian Robert McCarter, who has worked closely with me on this book as editor from start to finish.

Thanks to editors Megan Carey and Meredith Baber; designer Elana Schlenker; and Publisher Kevin Lippert of Princeton Architectural Press. Their intelligent, critical perspectives have reinforced the value of the longstanding working relationships that many of my colleagues and myself have enjoyed with the press.

Thanks to my assistants at MacKay-Lyons Sweetapple Architects: Lisa Morrison, who helped to organize the conference in 2011; Frances McGinnis, who began working on the book; and Lindsay Ann Cory, who brought it to fruition.

Father Michael Mitchell and the wardens of St. John's Anglican Church in Lunenburg generously provided the magnificent, carpenter gothic venue for the conference's three keynote lectures. The design/build efforts of Ghost Architectural Laboratory participants over the years have shaped the venue for the conference at our farm. Scott Geddes of Coco Pesto catering kept our bellies warm during that cold, wet June of 2011, as he has for many years of Ghosts.

No one who attended the conference will ever forget that first stormy morning when, just before Rick Joy's frozen fingers could start his presentation, we suddenly lost power. Within minutes my Acadian/Micmac friend, Barnell Duffenais, came flying over the hill with his truck and generator. We were soon back in business. When I thanked him he answered, "no problem buddy; the day that I can't help you out is the day I am dead." So, I like to say that in Nova Scotia, it is not the Calvary, but the Natives who come over the hill to save your butt.

Special thanks to Brigitte Desrochers, who believed in the importance of local architecture for our discipline, and the Canada Council for the Arts, for its generous support for both this book and the conference.

At the end of "Ideas in Things," I asked Juhani Pallasmaa for his advice on the future of the Ghost Lab. He suggested that it was time to take a break, because "it is the hospitality of your family that is the quality that makes Ghost special, and the most costly element." The conference, this book, our practice, and the paradise at the end of the earth that is the Ghost venue and our home have been sustainable mainly because of the unconditional support of my family—Marilyn, Renee, Alison, and Matthew. They are the ones who clean the toilets, haul the wood for the bonfire, and make our guests and friends feel at home.

And lastly, thanks to Darwin, the now departed bottle-fed lamb, who enjoyed peeing on the floor at the lectern, keeping the distinguished speakers down to earth.

—Brian MacKay-Lyons

Supplementary Image List

Deborah Berke Partners
Marianne Boesky Gallery, 51 top
Art Collector's Loft, 51 middle
Gracie Square Maisonette, 51 bottom

Marlon Blackwell Architect
Keenan Tower House, 57 top
Moore Honey House, 57 middle and bottom

Wendell Burnette Architects
Burnette Residence, 63 top
Field House, 63 middle
Desert Courtyard House, 63 bottom

Ghost Architectural Laboratory
Ghost Lantern,71

Rick Joy Architect
Tubac House, 85

Kéré Architecture
School Extension, 91

Richard Kroeker Design
Beaverbank, 99 top
Birch Bark Canoe, 99 second from top
Jig, 99 second from bottom
Cheticamp: Le Theatre du Petit Cercle, 99 bottom

Olson Kundig Architects
Chicken Point Cabin, 103 top and bottom
The Brain, 103 middle two

Lake | Flato Architects
Texas State Cemetery, 109 top
Porch House, 109 middle
Story Pool House, 109 bottom

MacKay-Lyons Sweetapple Architects
Cliff House, 115 top
Rubadoux Studio, 115 second from top
Howard House, 115 second from bottom
Sliding House, 115 bottom

The Miller Hull Partnership
Vancouver Community Library, 123

Patkau Architects
Tula House, 141 top
Linear House, 141 middle
Seabird Island School, 139 bottom

Rural Studio
Yancy Tire Chapel, 147 top
20K House II: Frank's House, 147 middle
Akron Boys and Girls Club, 147 bottom

Shim-Sutcliffe Architects
Craven Road Studio, 153

Studio 804
Modular 4, 159 top
Centre for Design Research, 159 middle
Wedding Chapel, 159 bottom

Peter Stutchbury Architecture
Deepwater Woolshed, 165

VJAA
Minneapolis Rowing Club Boat House, 171 top
Type Variant House, 171 bottom

Credits

Alvar Aalto Museum: 190

Steve Badanes: 80, 81

Benjamin Benschneider: 102, 103 bottom, 104 top, 105 top and bottom, 122, 123 top, 124, 125 bottom, 126 top, 127, 128–29

Marlon Blackwell: 58 left

Paul Crosby: 170, 171, 172, 173, 174–75

Mark Darley: 103 top and second from bottom

Deborah Berke Partners LLP: 54 top

Nicole Delmage: 71

James Dow: 140, 141, 142 left, 143, 144 left, 145, 152, 154 bottom, 155 top, 156–57

Casey Dunn: 109 bottom

Dwight Eschliman: 106–7

Steven Evans: 74 bottom

Chris Floyd: 54–55

Alex Fradkin: 219

Adam Friedberg: 51 bottom

Ghost Architecture Laboratory: 72 bottom

Bob Grundu: 153 middle and bottom

Hester & Hardaway: 109 top

Timothy Hursley: 56, 57 top, 58 right, 59, 60–61, 147, 149 top, 150–51

Richard Johnson: 57 middle and bottom

Kéré Architecture: 93 bottom, 95 top

Francis Kéré: 91 top, 94 left

Weneyida Kéré: 93 top, 95

Richard Kroeker: 98, 99 top, second from top, and bottom

Lake | Flato Architects: 110, 112–13

Jean-Luc Laloux: 84, 86 right, 87 bottom, 88–89

Dawn Laurel: 108, 111

Marlon Blackwell Architect: 58 top

Nic Lehoux: 123 bottom

Brian MacKay-Lyons: 72 left and right, 74 top

MacKay-Lyons Sweetapple Architects: 118

Steph MacKinnon: 70

The Miller Hull Partnership: 125 top, 126 bottom

Glenn Murcutt: 130, 132, 133, 134, 35, 136, 137, 138–39

Michael Nicholson: 164, 165, 166 top and bottom, 167 right, 168–69

Finn O'Hara: 153 top

Olson Kundig Architects: 104 bottom, 105 right

Frank Ooms: 109 middle

Erik-Jon Ouwekerk: 90, 91 bottom, 92, 96–97

Stamo Papadaki, *The Work of Oscar Niemeyer* (New York: Reinhold, 1950), 134: 189

Patkau Architects: 142 top, right, and bottom

Peter Stutchbury Architecture: 166 middle, 167 left

Jared Polesky: 82–83

Greg Richardson: 114, 115 top and bottom, 116, 117, 119, 120–21

Rick Joy Architect: 86 left and bottom, 87 top

Dan Rockhill, Courtesy Rockhill and Associates: 159 bottom

Dan Rockhill, Courtesy Studio 804: 158, 159 top and middle, 160 bottom, 161, 162, 163

Cherish Rosas: 7, 15, 16, 18, 23, 31, 41, 179, 185, 195, 201

Rural Studio, Auburn University: 146, 148, 149 bottom

Bill Sanders: 78–79

Jason Schmidt: 51 middle

Manuel Schnell: 76–77

Ferdinando Scianna: 205

Shim-Sutcliffe Architects: 154 top and left, 155 bottom

Arna Sisson: 99 second from bottom

Jamie Steeves: 73, 75, 115 second from top and bottom

Studio 804: 160 top

Catherine Tighe: 50, 51 top, 52 bottom, 53

Bill Timmerman: 62, 63, 64, 65, 66 top, 67 bottom, 68–69, 85

Paul Toman: 100, 101

Wendell Burnette Architects: 66 bottom, 67 top

Western Regional Archives, State Archives of North Carolina: 206

David Wild: 103 second from top

The Ghost Sessions
For a few days in June 2011, twenty-six distinguished architects and critics met to consider the current state of architecture at Ghost 13 on Brian MacKay-Lyons's farm on the Atlantic Coast of Nova Scotia.

Published by
Princeton Architectural Press
37 East Seventh Street
New York, New York 10003

Visit our website at www.papress.com.

Printed and bound in China by 1010 Printing International
18 17 16 15 4 3 2 1 First edition

Front Cover images, clockwise from top:
Benjamin Benschneider, Greg Richardson, and Jean Luc-Laloux
Back cover images, clockwise from top: Lorne Bridgeman, Steph MacKinnon, Cherish Rosas

Editor: Megan Carey
Associate Editor: Meredith Baber
Designer: Elana Schlenker

Special thanks to: Sara Bader, Nicola Bednarek Brower, Janet Behning, Carina Cha, Andrea Chlad, Barbara Darko, Ally Dawes, Benjamin English, Russell Fernandez, Will Foster, Jan Cigliano Hartman, Jan Haux, Mia Johnson, Diane Levinson, Jennifer Lippert, Emily Malinowski, Katharine Myers, Jaime Nelson, Jay Sacher, Rob Shaeffer, Sara Stemen, Marielle Suba, Paul Wagner, Joseph Weston, and Janet Wong of Princeton Architectural Press
—Kevin C. Lippert, publisher

Library of Congress Cataloging-in-Publication Data
Local architecture : building place, craft, and community / by Brian MacKay-Lyons ; edited by Robert McCarter.
— First edition.
pages cm
Includes bibliographical references.
ISBN 978-1-61689-128-2 (hardback)
1. Architecture—Environmental aspects—Congresses.
2. Architecture, Modern—21st century—Congresses. 3. Architectural design—Social aspects—Congresses. I. MacKay-Lyons, Brian, author. II. McCarter, Robert, 1955- editor of compilation. III. Ghost 13 (Symposium) (13th : 2011 : Nova Scotia)
NA2542.35.L63 2014
724'.7—dc23
2014007907